The
Grass Roots
Church

STEPHEN C. ROSE

The
Grass Roots
Church

A Manifesto for
Protestant Renewal

Introduction by Harvey Cox

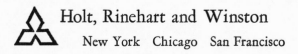

Holt, Rinehart and Winston
New York   Chicago   San Francisco

Grateful acknowledgment is made to the following for permission to include
selections from the books listed:

The Dial Press, Inc., for an excerpt from *The Fire Next Time* by James
Baldwin. Copyright © 1963, 1962 by James Baldwin.

The Macmillan Company for excerpts from *Letters to Young Churches: A
Translation of the New Testament Epistles* by J. B. Phillips (1947).

G. P. Putnam's Sons for excerpts from *The Presidential Papers* by Norman
Mailer. Copyright © 1960, 1961, 1962, 1963 by Norman Mailer.

Designer: Ernst Reichl
87560-0116
Printed in the United States of America

To the memory of one who once suggested
a direction and a responsibility,
the late Dr. Paul Austin Wolfe

Atonement, regeneration, the Holy Ghost, the love of our enemies, the cross and resurrection, life in Christ and Christian discipleship—all these things have become so problematic and so remote that we hardly dare anymore to speak of them. . . . So our traditional language must perforce become powerless and remain silent, and our Christianity today will be confined to praying for and doing right by our fellow man. Christian thinking, speaking, and organization must be reborn out of this praying and this action.

Dietrich Bonhoeffer

Contents

Introduction

Over a century ago an acute observer of the American scene, Alexis de Tocqueville, said:

"I am tempted to believe that what we call necessary institutions are often no more than institutions to which we have grown accustomed. In matters of social constitution the field of possibilities is much more extensive than men living in their various societies are ready to imagine."

In this book, Stephen Rose has taken a welcome step beyond the flood of recent literature that has criticized the existing forms of church life in America. He has boldly sketched out a "field of possibilities," a range of concrete suggestions on how we can alter the institutional shape of the churches to enable them to serve our emerging urban-technological society. He calls his suggestions for a revitalized and reformed church "evocative rather than rigid." Although his modesty is commendable, it is the very specificity of this book which makes it important. No longer will the strident defenders of our present denominational leviathans be able to say, as they often have in the past, that the advocates of renewal operate miles up in the stratosphere with no relationship to the structural realities of the American Church. This book puts the challenge where it cannot be avoided.

The mossbacks have been able to keep our present elephantine organizations lumbering along mainly because the critics who snipe at "denominationalism," "bureaucracy," or "the residential parish" have used hit-and-run guerrilla tactics, but have had no inclusive strategy and little agreement on what form of church life should replace the ones they were dismembering. Here is one vision, at least, of how the Church could organize its life, which has the virtue of being considerably different from the paleolithic way it is now. Yet at the same time this vision displays a thoroughgoing particularity and a degree of continuity with present patterns which preclude its being dismissed as a pipe dream. Whatever else one says about Rose's ideas, we *could* implement them starting now. If we wanted to.

The Grass Roots Church will draw fire from three sides. It will be opposed by those for whom any restructuring of church life seems presumptuous tinkering with an organism that God himself has ordained. The structural fundamentalists will not, or cannot, see that every form of church life has emerged within a given historical period and in response not only to the Gospel but to specifiable sociological pressures and possibilities. A century ago our grandfathers in the faith were released from the stifling dungeon of Scriptural literalism by the discovery and application of the principles of historical criticism to biblical texts. The result was a dynamic new view of the nature of religious truth and a method of gaining living access to truths whose antiquated garb had prevented us from encountering them. In this generation a comparable movement has begun to liberate us from our rigid and uncritical views of the form of church life. We see not only the wording of the message but the shape of the community as flexible, unfixed, and open to constant transmutation. The underlying theological insight here is that God lives for man *within* history, not beyond it in some fixed and timeless realm. Although there is "no shadow of turning" within God, his changelessness is not a platonic ideal but a fidelity within history, an unswerving loyalty to his human covenant partner amidst the ceaseless movement of men and nations. Therefore, faith in this God not only allows but requires a continuing reformation of Christian existence and church life.

Stephen Rose operates on this theological premise, although he does not make it explicit at every point. His book is faithful to the tradition of an *ecclesia semper reformanda*. But it takes the existing patterns of church life seriously as the point from which even the most radical sort of renewal must begin. This will arouse the ire of a second group of critics, those Christians for whom the only honest course left open today is to shake the dust of the Church from their feet and launch into a whole new orbit. These self-designated radicals believe that every moment used to renovate or repair existing Church institutions is a moment frittered away. To such people, Rose's book will sound like a whitewash, a too-easy apology for today's whore of Babylon, the bloated bureaucratic institutional Church.

If the weakness of the first group is theological—a nonhistorical doctrine of God and the Church—the blindness of the second is mainly sociological. They fail to see that nobody does anything today without some form of organization and, indeed, institutionalization. Look behind any successful march or picket line, the paradigm for open-throttled action in the world today, and you will find leadership, co-ordination, planning, phone calls—in short, a highly professional organization. The pseudoradical critics also fail to see that the Church in American society today represents institutional power. It has money, staff, buildings, investments. The genuine revolutionary, as opposed to the mere adventurist, will want to take these resources over, not just ignore them. One allegedly radical Christian had this brought forcibly to his attention when he was delivering a fiery denunciation of church buildings, declaring that if he had his way he would burn them all down and thus force the people of God to live an exposed existence in the world. Just as he finished, a Mississippi Negro rose and said that the only people he knew who wanted to burn churches down were the Ku Klux Klan.

The power and property of the church are in themselves more or less neutral. Church buildings can be used to plot demonstrations, insulate junior-high youth groups, provide a stage for experimental plays that no theater will risk, or encapsulate congregations in sin-proof vinyl. The same is true for the church's boards, agencies, investments, and pension plans. They can be used to perpetuate sterility or to crash through into radical identification with the forces of change and renewal in today's turbulent world.

Those who want to get in step with the God who changes things, with the One who exalts the poor and scatters the proud, must be concerned with the control and exercise of power. The fact is that in our society, some of this power—not much, admittedly, but some—now lies in the hands of the churches. A decision to ignore that power simply because of personal aversion or bad childhood memories of sanctimonious Sunday schools may be psychologically comprehensible, but it remains strategically indefensible. True, not everyone needs to devote his attention to recapturing the Church for the Gospel. But someone does. And this is not simply a matter of personal vocation or taste, although these enter into the choice. It is also a matter of calculated strategy on the part of those whose faith requires unconditional engagement in the struggle for a more human world.

The strength of this book is that it takes the Church seriously, but as an instrument, not as an end. Its orthodox, platonic critics will disapprove of the way it treats the Church as an expendable instrument in the sculpturing of a new humanity. Its adventurist critics will say that the Church is good for nothing, that it is not even a tool. There will be a third and more constructive group of critics, however, who will agree with the premises of the book but disagree with the proposals. I am sure Mr. Rose expects and desires this sort of criticism. It is this response which will move the discussion further along.

For example, some will want to see national Church bureaucracies retain a degree of autonomy, not simply out of sloth and greed, but because they often serve a prophetic function. Recent studies have shown that church executives who are insulated from direct lay control are usually more willing to take risky positions and support radical programs than those who must report immediately to lay constituencies. Say that this prophetic effectiveness is purchased at the price of lay participation if you will; still, it is one of the ways in which the Church has made possible a prophetic witness in recent years. Contrary to popular belief, people with tenure and pensions are sometimes more willing to support unpopular causes than the people who can be fired the next day. There is no reason, however, why Rose's emphasis on local responsibility could not be combined with a measure of power and autonomy at the top.

There will also be people who will insist that national Church organizations, simply because they represent a broader constituency, can bring constructive pressure to bear where it might not be generated in the area itself. The National Council of Churches' Mississippi Delta Ministry, which represents the very finest in what Rose hopes for the Church, would never have happened if the churches of Mississippi alone had been left to make the decision, no matter how united they were at the local level.

God often speaks to our provincial blindness today through the voice of the Church Universal. Latin American Christians remind us through the World Council of the parochialism of our interest in our poor, and point out to us that the evil structures of inter-American trade tend to keep whole nations on a starvation diet. The Pope sometimes makes the consciences of American Catholics uneasy in regard to race and war. The National Council of Churches criticizes American policy in Vietnam. It would be too bad if an anti-bureaucratic tidal wave swept away these avenues through which God calls the Church to repentance and mission from outside the local setting.

Still, Rose is perfectly right when he says that bureaucracy, as we now know it in the Church, must go. We must find ways to give the Church a series of more flexible, disposable organizational styles. We must pull churches in metropolitan areas away from their idiotic denominational divisions and tie them together around the life-and-death issues of the metropolis. Bureaucracy is headed for extinction, not only in the Church but in the society. Warren Bennis, of the Sloan School of Management at M.I.T., says that bureaucracy, with its well-defined hierarchy of authority, its standard procedures for dealing with all contingencies, its insistence on impersonality in work relations, and its emphasis on technical competence alone, is on the way out. It was the perfect form of organization for industrial development and for the Victorian era. It will not do for a period of accelerated scientific and social innovation. It is too rigid to cope effectively with the growing role of information feedback and ceaseless organizational self-analysis. Bennis foresees in industry the emergence of what he calls the "organic-adaptive structure" to replace bureaucracy. It will be based on different views of power, of man, and of the meaning of organization itself. It will maximize the inclusion of persons in decision-making processes which affect their lives. If our society is unable to devise these new styles of organization, Bennis predicts, it will inevitably decline into rigidity and ineffectuality. Classical bureaucratic forms of organization, though they must be credited with having brought us where we are today, must not be allowed to determine the next phase of cultural development. The future

demands *ad hoc* clusters, self-dismissing work teams, encourage-
ment for charismatic innovation, flexible lines of authority.

If the society itself needs a new style of social organization,
perhaps the Church can serve the world by experimenting in its
own life with unprecedented new forms of corporate existence.
These must maximize popular participation, keep the windows
open for unexpected new currents of innovation, and find
techniques by which a task can be tackled by people who then
dissociate and re-form in new patterns to attack another job.
Many of Stephen Rose's suggestions, coming from one who has
lived both within the existing structures and at the grass roots,
could move us in this direction. Those of us who yearn to pass
the Church on to their descendants the way we do family heir-
looms, and those for whom any effort to change the Church is a
treasonous betrayal of the needs of the world, had best close this
book immediately. In it they will find naught for their comfort
and much that will discomfit them. Those who wish, at least for
the moment, to crack the present stalemate and pour all the
Church has into God's jarring reconstitution of the world should
read on. They should read not simply to agree or disagree with
Stephen Rose, but to be goaded by his book to plot their own
plans for the seizure of power which must and will occur in the
Church.

HARVEY COX

Boston
August 4, 1966

Preface

Not many years ago, the great Christian thinker Reinhold Niebuhr summed up his attitude toward American Protestantism in one devastating word. The Church, he said, has become "trivial." He uttered that judgment despite the fact that, in the decade from 1950 to 1960, the American religious establishment was widely held to be in the midst of an unprecedented postwar revival.

During the first half of the 1960s, Niebuhr's verdict was repeated so often as to become almost trivial itself. A new rash of books hit the market, calling in quasi-prophetic tones for the renewal of the Church. We were inundated with visions of solemn assemblies, suburban captivity, comfortable pews, and ecumenical scandals on main street. Unrest *within* the Church became far greater than the outsider's concern *about* the Church. Scarcely a religious gathering was held without the presence of an iconoclastic jet-age circuit rider who, for an honorarium, flagellated the audience with visions of Christian irrelevance in our time. Others simply left the Church, convinced that bureaucracy and institutionalism had snuffed out all hope of renewal. The conclusion of both those who leave and those who remain to inveigh against the status quo is that the "structures" of the Church have become utterly irrelevant: the local congregation is obsolete; the denominations are hopelessly anachronistic; the minister's role is impossible, etc. But virtually no one has gone beyond these sad conclusions to suggest a comprehensive new structure for Protestantism. We are left with diagnoses aplenty, but scarcely a single prescription.

Now it is time for constructive proposals. That is the intention of this book. As editor of *Renewal* magazine, I have received many letters from ministers and laymen asking what can be done, beyond mere criticism, to move the Church from triviality to genuine involvement, not only with the world, but with the great traditions that once gave life to the Christian community. This book is my partial answer. It is presented in the form of a manifesto to all persons who are interested in the renewal of the Church.

I want to offer my thanks to the following persons for their very real assistance during the time that this book was being prepared, with the understanding that my gratitude does not implicate them in the results: Don Benedict, Helen Archibald, Peggy Way, the Board of Directors of the Chicago City Missionary Society, Jim McGraw, Roscoe Hill, Malcolm Boyd, Martin Marty, Jack Brennan, Robert Newman, Esq., and Lois Rose. I would also like to express my deep gratitude to Lois Olson and Mrs. Lillian Olson for their assistance in preparing the final manuscript. Finally I am most indebted to William Robert Miller for getting me started on this book and to Joseph E. Cunneen and Carolyn Means for getting me finished.

STEPHEN C. ROSE

Geneva, Switzerland
July 1966

Prologue

The Sunday-go-to-meeting days are over,
with their cloth-covered Christmas baskets for the parson,
their snap-clean petticoats, apple-polished cheeks
(Junior at attention next to sad-eyed Papa),
their lamb roasts with jelly, and deep-dish pies.

The family grace, the gilt-edged testaments worn
with devotion, the musty-smelling ten-year-old owl-faced
Plymouths chunking on dirt and barely tarred roads,
the local church college with two Ph.D.'s,
the one-room schoolhouse, one-track life, one religion,
just one wife, will of God, and woodshed whipping—
these and all the other half-real, half Norman Rockwell
intimations of something way back, when religion was
religion, and it was all right to take in Grandma when
Grandpa passed on—these are the dreams that white
Protestantism U. S. of A. (like a boy grown older and
moved to the big town) tries to recapture and cannot.

Pleasure evoked a tight-lipped smile, pain the solace of
warm family relations, another sort of pain the
damnation of emotions too deep to express. The body
was harnessed, ashamed of affection. And all who
offended were tossed to the world where pleasure wasn't
pleasure, joy not joy, to act out a parody of ancient

taboos. *Films came along to sustain the myth, with their*
rosy-cheeked virginal innocent blondes, their hands clasped
together, their eyes to the ground, and their gangling,
red-faced agricultural beaux, immigrant actors who changed
their names because America was, after all, a Protestant
nation. (Today the names are changed no more.)

If the Omnipotent God should somehow change, if He
should countenance a cocktail or laugh or somehow break
the mold, the Universe would crumble and Gaylord Ravenal,
the riverboat gambler, would win at last, with a puff on
his thin, black, heretical cigar and a flick of his
ill-gotten watch chain.

And then it came to pass that the Protestant population
of New York City ranked third—slightly outnumbered by
Jews and vastly outnumbered by Roman Catholics. And,
behold, a substantial portion of that Protestant strength
was not of that New England, Nieuw Amsterdam colony stock.
Oh, no, they were the children of slaves. And one realized
that the nation of austere farmers and occasional robber
barons was on its way to becoming nine-tenths urban
just two thousand years after that seminal Crime which seems
so hard to contemplate today, despite endowments,
cushioned pews, curricula, et cetera.

And so the Church will change or not, depending on the
blowing of the wind. . . . The Church will move as Jesus did
or cling to what it can't sustain. Authoritative frowns
of yesteryear may mellow into embarrassed grins of those
who dimly sense their business is to please old ghosts,
or not, depending on the blowing of the wind.

The
Grass Roots
Church

Chapter 1
Toward a New Structure
for Protestantism

1

It is no longer possible for Protestantism to survive in its present form. The present denominational organization of the churches is obsolete. Only a fraction of existing local congregations are equipped to meet the many requirements of the Christian community. And yet, despite the publication of countless criticisms of the Church in our time, no one has offered a constructive alternative to present patterns. This book is intended for those who have a sense of the criticisms, or at least see the deficiencies, and are ready to participate in a positive movement for the renewal of the Church.

During the coming years American Protestantism will be faced with harder and harder decisions. Already the foundations are shaking, theologically as well as institutionally. Membership in the churches has begun to decline in relation to population. The active involvement of persons who claim membership is also on the wane. Financial giving fails to keep pace with the costs of operating the Church as it is presently structured. There is unrest within the theological seminaries. As many as two-thirds of the students in seminaries state that they have no intention of entering the ministry unless the job description of the clergyman is changed radically. Active ministers, in larger and larger numbers, are saying they would leave their jobs if they could find other employment.

But it is not my intention to criticize what exists. Rather it is to offer a program for change, a program that could be adopted in any local congregation, by local congregations acting together, and—if the Spirit is willing—by the Church as a whole.

This, then, is a manual, a suggestion of basic theological and strategic guidelines for a positive renewal movement within Protestantism. It is for those who wish to move out of our present situation where stalemate, drift, and indecisiveness hold sway; those who are as concerned about the faithfulness of the Church to its own standards as about the relevance of the Church to the changing world at its doorstep. In short, this is written for those who would give partial or total assent to the following five assertions:

1. There must be increased participation by trained Christians in the fight to obtain social justice not only in the United States but throughout the world. Participation in the renewal movement is not denied to those who disagree concerning *how* the Church should deal with the explosive facts of racial upheaval, stark starvation, and incredibly rapid urbanization, but does exclude those whose eyes are closed to the fact that these problems exist and call for solution. The possibility of a renewal movement in America's churches is based on the hope of recovering a biblically prophetic insight into our cataclysmic times.

2. There must be equal emphasis placed on the necessity of a renewal of the traditional functions of the Church— the nurturing of community, the teaching of the faith, and the pastoral and preaching ministries. Thus, in proposing a new structure for Protestantism, the priority is not on supplementary structures that will enable the "far out" clergy to experiment at the edges of the religious institution. I do not propose an occasional "Christian coffee house" here, a maverick ministry to the poor there, or a series of *ad hoc* activities carried out without the knowledge and consent of most church members. Such an approach only shields us from the depths of the Protestant sickness. The first persons to see this should be the *avant garde* within the churches. Of all people, they should realize that such scattershot renewal is, at best, partial and, at worst, a concession on the part of the status quo, anxious to please the prophets in order to keep them confined to the periphery.

3. An effective renewal movement will be radically ecumenical. Members of such a movement must be willing to forsake loyalty to their denominations when the denominational structures impede the development of united, ecumenical mission, particularly at the local level. The aim of the renewal movement will not be primarily the merger of existing denominations but rather the transformation of denominationalism itself. If there is any future for the denominations, it lies in their serving as an ecumenical resource to congregations which agree to act cooperatively at the local and metropolitan level.

4. The renewal movement must emphasize the need for a new theology which can be developed within the context of the Church as it is, rather than in the isolated corridors of the seminaries and the technical pages of scholarly journals. At the same time the movement must allow for theological diversity, not only in the name of tolerance, but in

the name of honesty as well. Insistence on strict theological consensus is becoming a ruse by which to avoid genuine ecumenical encounter. We should aim rather for a Church in which many theological insights are accessible to the total membership.

5. The renewal movement will accept three general principles which will form the basis for the development of a constructive strategy:

a) the priority of local ecumenicity; b) the necessity of combining existing forms of Church government to allow for decentralization, increased participation at the local level, and the development of a streamlined structure at regional and national levels; c) the need for a redefinition of Church membership in terms of "basic membership" (through baptism, confirmation, etc.) and "functional membership" (through voluntary participation in specific areas of Christian witness).

2

During the course of this book, I shall use three terms to indicate what I believe are the functions of the Church. The traditional description of the Church's threefold ministry is summed up in the Greek words *diakonia, koininia,* and *kerygma. Diakonia* refers to the obligation of the Church to be a servant people, but we have made the deacons in our local congregations into what is, at best, an internal service organization. *Koininia* signifies the imperative that the Church be a community of love, but it implies nothing about the structure of this community. *Kerygma* refers to the central task of the Church, which is the proclamation or preaching of the Good News of the Gospel. However, the very notion of *kerygma* has been subverted by the Church's inability to provide a context in which genuine preaching is possible. There may be a time when we can revive these terms without doing offense to their meaning. But, for the moment, I propose to develop three alternative concepts to describe the functions of a renewed Church. They are *chaplaincy, teaching,* and *abandonment.*

Chaplaincy refers to the traditional and, generally speaking, ordained ministry of the Church. It embraces the task of establishing a meaningful worship life, providing pastoral care and preaching the Word of God. Chaplaincy is the work for which most seminary students today are trained, but which they scarcely have time to perform when they take on the Jack-of-all-trades job of the contemporary minister. Chaplaincy is to be understood as the priestly, liturgical, kerygmatic ministry of the Church.

The second function of the Church is *teaching.* St. Paul wisely informs us that some are called to prophesy, some to preach, some to counsel, and some to teach. But with a passion for inefficiency, Protestantism has sought to make teaching a sort of fifth trade of a clergy that is already overburdened with responsibility. We build elaborate educational wings for our churches and staff them, for the most part, with persons who lack ability as teachers. The minister today who takes teaching seriously is well advised to forget all other obligations, because teaching is a full-time job. Along with chaplaincy, teaching is a traditional function of the Church. I shall seek to demonstrate in the following pages that the present structure of Protestantism works *against* the performance of both these functions.

Beyond chaplaincy and teaching, the third function of the Church can be described as *abandonment.* Abandonment has two meanings. It applies to everything the Church does in addition to chaplaincy and teaching. In its first meaning, abandonment implies a literal vacating of the premises—

abandoning a location, leaving a building. Abandonment
suggests the capacity of an institution—the Church—to give
up all programs, buildings, and financial commitments that
are peripheral to the root ministries of chaplaincy and teaching. Abandonment is indeed the only rationale for chaplaincy and teaching. Without it there is neither.

Abandonment also implies a giving up of one's life for
another. It suggests the spirit of Jesus' request that we take
no thought for the morrow. It means a giving up of one's self
to a task, a pursuit, a goal. Understood in this way, abandonment has two strategic implications. First, the laity is called
to abandon itself to the needs of the world. Insofar as the
Church is a servant Church, it will depend increasingly on
the training of laymen to carry their faith into the complex
corners of modern existence, there to give witness in action
to the radical implications of the Gospel. If the Church were
doing its job of chaplaincy and teaching adequately, it would
not constantly have to set up professional institutions to perform the very tasks that a trained laity could accomplish far
more adequately in the context of their normal existence.
The present tendency is for the frustrated clergy to take over
the Church's social-action responsibility. This only postpones
the day when the laity will be recognized as the prophetic
arm of the Christian community. Certainly one object of
the renewed Church is to produce a revolutionary laity. This
means that the teaching structures of the Church will have
to be placed so that they can serve laymen where they are.
It means, too, that Church membership will be defined in
terms of both confession of faith and involvement in specific
forms of abandonment.

Abandonment to the world also requires a considerable
degree of institutional flexibility. Certainly the national denominations will need to become far more flexible if they are
to play a part in the renewal movement. It may seem strange

to suggest that renewal could take place without denominational leadership and/or cooperation. My only response is that if the denominations remain intransigent, set in their own ways, unwilling to give up cherished bureaucratic precedents, they will indeed have to be bypassed. A later chapter will deal with the ways in which this bypassing might occur. At this point we can say that the principle of abandonment involves the ability of a locally administered, ecumenical church to move rapidly to meet community needs, to respond favorably to experimental thrusts, and to permit interested laymen and ministers to develop a variety of new forms of gathering, of living together, of communal witness.

3

The renewed Church will embody a structural distinction between chaplaincy, teaching, and abandonment. In subsequent chapters, I hope to sustain the point that the vast majority of local denominational congregations are not equipped to perform all three of these ministries. Nor is it necessary that they should. What I shall outline is a cooperative ministry of clusters of churches in a local area. Within such clusters chaplaincy would be performed in some of the buildings that house today's local congregations. These facilities would be staffed by men and women who specifically see their vocation as chaplaincy—that is, preaching, counseling, and the performance of the sacramental ministry of the Church. They would be the locus of the worshiping Church as no denominational local congregation of today can hope to be. There could be neighborhood facilities for pastoral counseling. Those called to counsel would counsel. Those called to preach would preach. There would be a diversity of worship services to meet the diversity of the human soul. The outsider could avail himself of the resources of chaplaincy without feeling the typical pressure which today's local congregation places on him to join, join, join. At the same time the specialized ministries within the local and metropolitan setting would serve as centers of Christian apologetics far more effectively than today's congregations.

The cooperative ministries would support one or more round-the-week educational facilities staffed by professionals and trained volunteers whose talent lies in teaching. Such facilities at the local level would be supported ecumenically; they would be free to develop their own curricula; those called to teach would be free to do so. In particular, there could be in every residential area a specific, open facility where an ongoing course of adult training in theology, the Bible, and the social and cultural implications of Christianity would be available. A full-fledged teaching ministry would replace the moralizing and off-the-cuff instruction that often passes for Sunday School education today.

Within the proposed structure, the local congregation would be redefined. In effect, all cooperating Christians (including Protestants, Orthodox, and Catholics when possible) in a given locality would be members of a cooperative ministry which would *be* the local congregation. The facilities which house the local denominational congregations of today would be used by the cooperative ministry as centers of chaplaincy, teaching, and abandonment. Thus, within the cooperative ministry, there would develop a new form of congregation. An individual would have basic membership in the cooperative ministry. Then he would assume a specific responsibility within the total ministry—either by assisting in the resource ministries of chaplaincy and teaching or in the various forms of abandonment, which, as we shall see, can be local, metropolitan, national, or international.

It will be seen that I am advocating a meaningful ecumenism, a local, grass roots movement which stresses responsibility where people actually live and work. In a sense, I am calling for the death of the denominations as we know them. I am not suggesting a merger of denominations into a centralized super-Church. Mergers at the top are hardly likely to reduce the costs and duplication that already haunt Protestant policy. Nor is there any likelihood that a merger at the top will have more than an antagonistic effect on local churches. I am advocating a sweeping away of an already formidable Protestant superstructure. The renewed Church would seek to operate from a decentralized base. It would adopt a new polity forged by existing local congregations in concert with one another and a new specialization which would enable many acting together to accomplish what separated Christianity finds impossible to do.

4

It is becoming obvious in our time that urbanization will define the nature of all future society. Virtually every important segment of the American economy is centered in the new metropolis—heavy industry, the production of consumer goods, transportation, communications, leisure-time facilities. And today the city is threatened as never before, not only by the inherent problems that result from massive concentrations of population, but by a standardized, thoughtless tide of commercial culture, tied to profit and lowest-common-denominator banality.

It may be true, as Harvey Cox suggests in his recent book *The Secular City,* that urbanization offers man an escape from the oppressive uniformity of the gossip-ridden small town, but this new freedom also enables him to be unconcerned about the total metropolis. The isolation of urban man can be, and already is proving to be, fatal to the city.

The dominant pattern in the metropolis is one of utter unconcern about the environment beyond the immediate walls of one's home and office. Some observers have noted that it is impossible for one to be neighborly in the modern metropolis, in the traditional sense of the neighborhood. One's communal involvements, one's friendships, one's commitments will necessarily be selective. But this relatively new possibility of isolation also "frees" one to care about nothing. Thus the residents of the secular city of choice may be successfully immunized against the travails of the city of necessity. It is, at the least, premature to claim that the impersonal patterns of the emerging metropolis are an entirely positive phenomenon. Whether they can offer a viable substitute for traditional communities based on kinship, local loyalty, and geographical proximity is a question of grave importance. Rather like the speaker in Matthew Arnold's *Dover Beach,* the fragmented man of the emerging metropolis tends to see the world as a place that

> Hath really neither joy, nor love, nor light,
> Nor certitude, nor peace, nor help for pain;
> And we are here as on a darkling plain
> Swept with confused alarms of struggle and flight,
> Where ignorant armies clash by night.

Metropolitan man senses the confused alarms and recoils from them—seeking security, afraid of change, living in a precarious world on the brink of ——— what? He hardly wants to know.

At the same time, it is clear that the man of the future will need to deal in a sophisticated way with structures and machines that threaten to reduce him to a cog or cipher. Urbanization produces the megalopolis whose residents are, of necessity, affected by highly technical decisions. Such a prospect is both confusing and challenging. The Church must be restructured so that it can tie together the diverse insights needed to master metropolitan life. It must provide urban man with the spiritual and ethical tools he needs to meet the challenge. Armed with a renewed vision of the Gospel, it may be the only institution that can.

The greatest threat posed by urbanization is the loss of a sense of participation by the individual in the basic decisions of life. This helps to explain the militant demands for "home rule" and self-determination that one hears from the ranks of ghetto residents who have formed community organizations.

Thus one primary *sociological* guideline for the Church in the new metropolis is a recognition of the need for self-determination and the restoration of local responsibility to its membership. To paraphrase a point that Robert Nisbet makes in his book *The Quest for Community*, the Church must seek to diversify and decentralize its own administrative operations and to relate these as closely as possible to the forms of spontaneous association which are the outgrowth of human needs and desires. The late missionary Roland Allen reminds us that the early Church did not rely on a large institutional superstructure, removed from local communities, to insure its expansion. In fact the missionary methods of St. Paul were radically different from those employed by today's Protestant denominations. Allen suggests several principles which Paul followed as he sought to establish the early Church:

(1) All teaching to be permanent must be . . . so capable of being grasped and understood that those who have once received it can retain it, use it, and hand it on . . .

(2) All organization . . . must be of such a character that it can be understood and maintained. It must be an organization of which people see the necessity: it must be an organization which they can and will support. It must not be so elaborate or so costly that small and infant communities cannot supply the funds necessary for its maintenance . . .

(3) All financial arrangements . . . should be such that the people themselves can and will control and manage their own business independently of any foreign subsidies.

(4) A sense of mutual responsibility of all the Christians for one another should be carefully inculcated and practiced . . . *

The proposed structure which I shall elaborate takes into account the fundamental wisdom (and unquestionable effectiveness) of St. Paul's missionary methods: the direct training of the Church membership to assume specific tasks; the necessity of an organizational pattern that is simple, direct, and unencumbered by inflexible habits and procedures; the need for a financial policy which enables the indigenous Church to act freely and for which the local membership assumes maximum responsibility; and, above all, a sense of mutual responsibility that is truly ecumenical in scope.

Even though the following chapters are concerned primarily with the development of the Church structure I have outlined, it will be recognized that structure alone is scarcely *the* key to Protestant renewal. There must be the liberating action of the Holy Spirit, enabling us to recover the sustain-

* *Missionary Methods: St. Paul's or Ours?* (Grand Rapids, Mich.: Eerdmans paperback, 1962), p. 151.

ing insights of the Gospel. There must be an intelligible attempt to define the contemporary meaning of biblical truth. Hopefully, neither of these imperatives will be lost in the effort to move toward a more positive structure for Protestantism.

Chapter 2
The Need for
Institutions

1

The basic obstacle facing the renewal movement is the tendency to confuse *institutions* and *institutionalism*. The Church is necessarily an institution. The question is one of how the institution is organized, of whether it is flexible enough to adapt to new situations. The institution that takes renewal seriously makes continual provision for its own transformation from one form into another. Institutionalism, on the other hand, is the loss of flexibility, the tendency to cling to old patterns, the stubborn refusal to change. The distinction should be clear enough, but there are those within Protestantism whose discouragement with present structures is so great that they have made institutions rather than institutionalism the archenemy. This has enabled preservers of the status quo to make the common charge that many critics of the Church want to throw out the baby with the bath water. The anti-institutional approach enables persons who defend the *institution* to avoid the more relevant charge that the Church has become mired in the mud of *institutionalism*.

The germ of the anti-institutional attack can be found in a terse sermon, delivered in 1963 by the Reverend Gordon Cosby, minister of the Church of the Saviour, Washington, D.C.* It seemed ironical at the time that the minister of one of the foremost examples of a renewed congregation would have advocated the complete overthrow of practically all present Church structures, but he did. "Just a few weeks ago," said Cosby, "I crossed a line in my thinking. Now I am convinced that the institutional structures that we know are not renewable. Even when there is renewal (and this goes on in many congregations) the stance of the Church almost always remains the same—a stance which is contrary to the very nature of a church committed to mission." At the outset, Cosby explained that he had reached his decision with reluctance: "The Holy Spirit is still at work in the old structures. People still get converted in them, and personal growth takes place in them. One reason it has been so difficult for me to come to the conclusion stated above is that I, myself, came to know Jesus Christ through the old structures. This reproach has been thrown at me time and time again . . . [but] this is not the way it seems to me God will work in our time."

Cosby then proceeded to define the Church as "mission." The congregation should express its life "in the world."

"Much more important than the . . . structures of a Church in dispersion is the spirit of the people. We still have to have the *charisma*—gift of the Spirit."

Cosby went on to claim that "It is in the seminaries and

* Reprinted in *Who's Killing the Church?, A Renewal Reader*, edited by Stephen C. Rose, 1966, pp. 53-58.

churches that we are most apt to discover the people who can develop the new shapes of the Church. . . . Of all people they are the ones who should know that the present structures do not work, that they are irrelevant. . . . Christ made himself vulnerable to the world. The Church is to be vulnerable to the world. It is to take the shape that the world needs. . . . The Church is in the world to die, not to develop power structures that protect it from any form of crucifixion."

Cosby suggested three possibilities:

I think we ought to be open to the giving up of all professional ministries. It may be that I ought to earn my livelihood another way. Perhaps all the ministers of a congregation should be engaged in a tent-making ministry and do their job in the life of the world.

. . . I think our present real estate serves us, but I think that a pilgrim people ought always to be open to the possibility of giving up all its real estate. . . . The Church was the Church during the most vibrant period of its life, several hundred years, without real estate.

Another possibility is that the Church might carry out its mission through small bands of people, just two or three or four or five, who would live out their lives in the midst of the world of business, the world of government, the world of the mass media, the medical world, the educational world—out there where they are making their tents, earning their living.

Cosby made it clear that he was not talking about "little functional groups related to the local congregation." The small mission groups would "*be* the local congregation." He took as the scriptural basis for this notion of the congregation Christ's avowal that "Where two or three are gathered together in my name, there am I in the midst of them."

Cosby anticipated the argument that such a Church structure would minimize the role of the ordained minister as
preacher and administrator of the sacraments: "What does
it mean," he asked, "to congregate in the name of Christ?
It means to have been baptized into His nature. . . . The
congregation is a people to whom the Word of God is
preached and to whom the sacraments are administered.
. . . Anyone who is appointed by that community of faith
may do them." Nor was Cosby concerned about the effect
that his plan, if realized, would have on the present structures of Protestantism.

Somebody says, "Aren't you afraid of what this would do?
Everything would go to pieces. Thousands of new congregations.
Hundreds of new denominations." Such a prospect does not
worry me a bit, not one tiny bit. It is only part of what I see as I
try to discover the shape of the future.
The congregation of the future will live under a common
discipline. It will take seriously not just the "gathering," but the
going forth. Think of the freedom such a congregation would
have—its mobility, with almost none of the paraphernalia or
baggage of the institution—with all of its energy available for its
mission.
. . . We would encounter one another as people who have left
their fortified positions and now only vaguely remember those
strong and solid houses we once inhabited. We would really be
a pilgrim people—a tent-dwelling people. We would recognize
one another with an inward recognition.

2

The first question, of course, is whether Cosby is, as suggested earlier, anti-institutional. Perhaps he is not. He
suggests the rejection of practically every Protestant form

and structure, but he presupposes the creation of a new and more flexible institution. No one can argue with Cosby's hope that a substantial number of highly disciplined, flexible missionary cadres might emerge from today's local congregations. But is the hope justified? It is important to understand that Cosby speaks from the perspective of the Church of the Saviour where, under his leadership, a small congregation has reached a phenomenal level of participation. The congregation requires extensive education as a prerequisite of membership. The members are organized into specialized mission groups, with such responsibilities as the operation of a coffee house and a retreat center. Financial giving to the church and individual commitment on the part of the membership are exceptionally high.

It is from this vantage point, I believe, that Cosby gains his faith in the power of the Spirit to transform a sinful people into a highly dedicated congregation. But this is not enough, in terms of Cosby's sermon. The very notion of loyalty to the institutional programs of the church is, he suggests, misguided. And so he arrives at the conclusion that even the congregation of the Church of the Saviour is not "in the world" in any relevant sense.

One visits the church and is amazed to hear accounts of individual transformations that have taken place among the members, but one also sees that the social impact of the congregation is no greater than that of considerably less disciplined local churches.* A curious paradox is evident. Jesus said, "The well have no need of a physician." The remark can be taken on two levels: No human being can exist without a "physican," because no human being, apart from the sustenance of God, is "well." Or, it can mean that there

---

* Elizabeth O'Connor, *Call to Commitment* (New York: Harper & Row, 1963), is a sympathetic account "from the inside" of the development of the Church of the Saviour.

are some who are healed, who are "well" enough to carry on without the sustaining help of a "physician." In a sense the congregation of the future, in Cosby's view, is made up of the "well." If the missionary cadres of which he speaks have need of a physician, this fact will still not prevent them from fulfilling a high degree of commitment one to another and to their specific mission in the world. They are sufficiently "cured" to be able to "venture out." I would agree that it is highly desirable that such groups as Cosby describes be a primary expression of the renewed Church. But to suggest that these groups can emerge out of nothing, as it were, and that they could be sustained without the resources provided by a broader and more diverse fellowship borders on a kind of perfectionism.

Persons attracted by what would appear to be an "instant relevance" would seem to be the most likely to respond to Cosby's vision and the least capable, in terms of maturity, of realizing his ideal in practice. Also, there is a real and debilitating tension between the piety that seems called for and the necessity for compromise when one takes seriously the rough-and-tumble of politics, education, business, etc. Cosby's quite valid critique of Protestant *institutionalism* escapes the arduous task of sorting out what must be jettisoned and what must be strengthened as we seek to renew Protestant *institutions*. As one who has spent years trying to create a valid form of the Church, he is right to complain of the smugness and lack of dedication that pervade so much of Protestantism. It is the cry of one who can honestly see no determinative force for renewal within the present structures.

3

Having dwelt at such length with Cosby's suggestive re-
marks, it would be dishonest not to explain more fully why
they seem inadequate. I believe there are two main forces
for renewal within Protestantism. The first is that represented by Cosby, the approach that rejects present institutions and moves forward in fragmented fashion into the
promise and pain of the world. In various ways, the Cosby
approach toward renewal is becoming a pattern at certain
points in the Church. In some cases congregations have split
on various theological and social issues, and the result has
been the formation of new congregations (often without
buildings) which seek to mirror more fully the relevance of
the biblical faith. I have little doubt that if this continued
splitting off of the "dedicated minority" from the status quo
church as the *only* strategy of renewal is encouraged, it will
occur increasingly throughout the Church as a whole. If I
read the writings of an influential theological thinker like
Johannes Hoekendijk correctly, this splitting-off strategy is
seen as both valid and salutary. Certainly the idea of a dedicated minority is not new and, in the past, it has functioned
well as an approach to change. It is at present the most likely
pattern for a renewal movement among the American Protestant churches.

The second approach to renewal is the one that is partially
outlined in this book. It assumes that the era of sectarianism
within Protestantism is over and that ecumenicity is a more
constructive path than fragmentation. It assumes that sects in
our increasingly pluralistic society are likely to resort to self-
righteousness and subtle but real forms of otherworldliness

in order to gain a certain self-definition. It also assumes that it is highly improbable that a disorganized sectarian pro-liferation of self-proclaimed "creative minorities" can be the chrysalis of the renewal of the whole Church. The idea of giving up on the institutional Church is most tempting to me and to many others. I say that precisely this giving up *may* have to happen eventually. But I say with equal inten-sity that to adopt this giving up as the basic approach *now* is to eliminate a crucial step in the process of change, namely, the step of proposing a concrete alternative to the status quo. It gives up on the institution without trying to change it. It proclaims the revolution before there are more than a hand-ful of revolutionaries. It tends to blur the issues at stake, since most Church splits today are based more on *sub rosa* issues than on the honest definition of theological and social disagreements. I agree entirely with the anti-institutional renewalists that there is no point in trying to resuscitate the denominations in their present form. But I ask them in all honesty whether they are willing to invest at least some of their energies in a truly ecumenical renewal movement that seeks not to siphon off an "elite" from existing congrega-tions, but to transform the structures and lives of these congregations. If they are willing to do this and find it of no avail, then they can move on to fight the institution, and they will have more allies than they can now claim.

Perhaps some souls will emerge from the present wilder-ness in ultimate desperation or charismatic faith to actually begin the Church that would "really be a pilgrim people," capturing some of the spirit which seems to have pervaded the New Testament Church. I would argue, though, that the early Church need not be the only model on which to base the Church of the future. The first Christians built their fellowship—at least to some extent—around the notion that

the return of Christ to earth, the final judgment, was im-
minent. Whatever their merits, the successive changes that
have taken place within the structure of the Church have
been a response to the historical moment, to the apprehension
by Christians of what God intends the Church to be at a
given time.

The Protestant principle means the continual imperative
to be responsive to the present will of God under which the
Church is called to live. It was this principle that led Luther,
Calvin, and the other Reformers to break with the Roman
Catholicism of the Renaissance. The same principle may be
said to have informed the ministry of John Wesley in the
eighteenth century. And I would maintain that the very
same principle is at work within the Roman Catholic
Church today, as it seeks to respond to the pioneering vision
of the late Pope John XXIII.

This book seeks a responsible application of the Protestant
principle to the current institutional difficulties of Protestantism. To adopt a purely sectarian approach—the split-off approach might be an appropriate description—is to ignore the
Protestant principle which, while critical of all forms of institutionalism, sees the necessity for institutions. Indeed,
while we often speak of the Protestant principle, we rarely
practice it. And in the context of Protestantism today, such
a failure to practice is less than responsible.

The denominations of the Church, while diminishing in
strength and influence, are still formidable. They command
great financial resources, including almost unbelievable investments in corporations and real estate. It is highly unrealistic to assume that the power inherent in the current
denominational enterprise will not be used in some way, and
it is highly irresponsible to forfeit at least the possibility of
some influence on how this power is used. Actually, if

Church power were used responsibly, the result would be a far greater social relevance (Cosby's goal) than now exists. If church homes for the aged were truly integrated, if church housing were truly innovative, if church schools were truly imaginative, if church funds were wisely invested, in short if the great institutional machinery of Protestantism were deployed with a certain flair for strategy and service, we should accomplish many aims that we often conceive to be beyond the institutional capacity of the Church. In the best of all possible worlds, the Church might not have as much real estate as it now owns, but it owns this property, and we have a responsibility to do something about it, even if what we finally do is to sell or give it away. The Church invests in corporations, and it is our responsibility to question these investments and to develop a voice within the power structures of the Church's financial units. We could go on. But suffice to say that we owe the Church the obligation of trying to develop institutional relevance before summarily jettisoning the institution. We must, at least for now, place renewal and restructuring ahead of total rejection of the institution.

The Protestant principle means a dedication to the task of renewal in the sense that James Baldwin defines it in a passage from *The Fire Next Time*:

. . . It is the responsibility of free men to trust and celebrate what is constant—birth, struggle, and death are constant, and so is love, though we may not always think so—and to apprehend the nature of change, to be able and willing to change. I speak of change not on the surface but in the depths—change in the sense of renewal. But renewal becomes impossible if one supposes things to be constant that are not—safety, for example, or money, or power. One clings then to chimeras, by which one can only be betrayed . . .*

* *The Fire Next Time* (New York: The Dial Press, 1963), p. 106.

Renewal is nothing more or less than the process of affirming what can be affirmed, changing to meet new contingencies, and casting off the protective garments that are no longer part of what St. Paul calls "the whole armor of God."

Therefore you must wear the whole armor of God that you may be able to resist evil in its day of power. . . . Take your stand with Truth as your belt, Righteousness as your breastplate, the Gospel of Peace firmly on your feet, Salvation as your helmet and in your hand the sword of the Spirit, the Word of God. Above all be sure you take Faith as your shield.*

Renewal implies a willingness to live in the now, to grasp the moment with passion, perception, and courage. But we are also to celebrate the things that are constant. Renewal is not possible if our belief is that God is an inactive Upstairs Accountant who spends His days recording the new memberships gained by the churches in the various geographical areas of the world where they happen to be present. Renewal presupposes the God of the Bible. It demands an openness on the part of the Church. It thus points to risk. Norman Mailer has written:

. . . If we are to speak of the shadows which haunt America today, the great shadow is that there is a place for everybody in our country who is willing to live the way others want him to. . . . Yes, there is a place for everybody now in the American scene except for those who want to find the limits of their growth by a life which is ready to welcome a little danger as part of the Divine cocktail.**

* J. B. Phillips, trans., "The Letter to the Christians at Ephesus," *Letters to Young Churches: A Translation of the New Testament Epistles* (New York: Macmillan, 1947), p. 109.
** *The Presidential Papers* (New York: G. P. Putnam's Sons. 1963), p. 21.

What sort of cocktail is American Protestantism willing to drink in the age of the metropolis? I suggest the answer does not lie in sweeping away every vestige of the present structure. We have yet to challenge the present institution with the specifics of renewal. Let us do so, and let us see what happens.

Chapter 3
The Need for
Change

1

Once the renewal movement has reached agreement on the positive value of institutions, provided they are flexible and sufficiently defined to serve their stated purposes, it is necessary to develop a basic argument for changing the institutional patterns that presently exist. Recent literature on the Church has concentrated on the *inadequacy* of what now exists. Gibson Winter has shown the difficulty that current Protestant structures face in serving the metropolis. Martin Marty has offered telling arguments to demonstrate the negative effects of denominationalism on Church mission. It is not my intention to add to this body of criticism—not because the criticism is wrong, but because I believe we can now move beyond it. Perhaps the best argument for changing the structures of Protestantism is that the present form of the Church seems unable to speak to the outsider, or to vitally involve those who are already on the "inside."

Consider first the outsider. Of course, there are those on
the outside who feel they are not "good" enough to become
members. They see the Church not as a community of the
forgiven but rather as a league of the unforgiving. There
are also some in our society who steadfastly refuse to involve
themselves in anything that does not serve the most crass
demands of personal self-interest. One might point out, in
addition, that a substantial number of persons who once
joined the Church out of a desire for social advantage or
"belonging" no longer "need" the Church as a launching
pad for their status seeking. Certainly if the Church is truly
the Church it is not likely to be a popular organization. The
Gospel is a scandal to those who maintain humanistic illusions about the perfectibility of man and the self-sufficiency
of the world. And the Christian community, when it exists,
is always a potential threat to the status quo. That is why
the Church is never more loved by the powerful than when
it is mired under the weight of its own institutionalism.

2

But it may be that the most telling argument for changing
both the structure and emphases of Protestantism comes
from another group of outsiders who could be called the
"unchurched remnant." These are persons who regret the
fact that they must stand outside.

I am not referring to persons who leave the ecclesiastical
establishment in a burst of rage over personalities or minor
issues of programming. I am speaking generally of young
men and women, brought up in the Church, who leave at
the first opportunity. I am talking about nominal Protestants
who consistently refuse the invitation to attend church or
who come only at Christmas and Easter. Generally speak-

ing, these are persons who reject the Church for perfectly plausible reasons. If we were to draw a portrait of such a person, he might have the following characteristics:

1. He is concerned about social issues. He feels the Church is not.
2. He is busy and seeks to be a good steward of his time. He feels his time is better spent elsewhere than "in church."
3. He is tasteful and discriminating. He feels that the Church is trivial and banal.
4. He feels that he can practice what religion he has without joining and participating in the activities of the Church.
5. He cares about big issues—life and death, the meaning of work and vocation, the nature of personal relationships. He does not feel that the Church provides resources for meeting or even discussing these problems.

Clearly this person is not the sport-shirted golfer who deposits wife and children at the church door each Sunday to enjoy a few free hours on the links. Nor is he a rabid atheist, though he may be more agnostic than Christian. He may be educated; indeed the rising educational level of Americans seems to suggest that Church membership in the future will need to embody greater intellectual challenge. He is concerned about "doing good things without being goody." He is not a bored person, but Church tends to bore him.

His case against church attendance may be summed up under three headings: failure of teaching, inappropriate demands on time and talent, and offenses against taste.

Our composite nonchurchman is interested in the question of life's meaning. But one who contributed to this composite picture sums up his impression of the Church as follows: "You walk in and out on Sunday morning. Hats are about the only thing you *can* talk about. There seems to be no chance for debate or the discussion of real issues. It is not the people's fault. They're not uninterested in these things. But in church the set-up is such that you get a negative view. Even if things weren't dull, they would seem so."

This image is partly due to a lamentable failure of local congregations to do more than sporadic work in the field of adult education. Only a handful of congregations have significant programs of study and discussion. The Church of the Saviour in Washington, D.C., requires laymen to take the equivalent of a year's seminary training before becoming members. But this stands in stark contrast to thousands of congregations which neither require lay training nor build voluntary programs of education into their structure. Only a tiny percentage of lay persons are invited to retreats and special courses where they are exposed to the deep meaning of biblical faith and its implication for the modern world. *The present structure of Protestantism effectively shields most laymen, not to mention outsiders, from the best the Church has to offer.*

It would be interesting to receive the answers of Protestant congregations to the following questions, designed to reveal the extent to which they serve as a resource to their members.

a) Is there a program of adult education, beyond a few sporadic study groups? Is attendance required before one can become a member?

b) Does the church provide courses of study on the city, world peace, theology, death, professional ethics, etc.?

c) Are such courses publicized and open to the public?

d) Who in the congregation is trained to provide such courses?

e) What per cent of the congregation's time and money is spent on adult education?

Let us assume that our hypothetical nonchurchman has perhaps ten or fifteen hours a week to devote to activities beyond job or home. If he were to take seriously the scriptural injunction that he observe one full day of rest, his time would be even further limited. Assuming he wishes to attend church at all, he has, in most cases, only one choice— the eleven o'clock hour on Sunday morning. For metropolitan man, this single hour is an unfortunate chronological basket into which to throw all of one's eggs. It may be appropriate to an agrarian society, but is it appropriate, practically or theologically, to the new metropolis? In a specialized society, where night shifts are common, and nurses and bus drivers work on weekends, insistence on this time as the only fitting moment for public worship is both anachronistic and discriminatory. No individual congregation could hold enough services to meet the time problems of man in the city, but a cooperative ministry of several congregations could. There are those who argue that a move away from the "sacred" Sunday hour is a dire blow to the notion that it is *then* that the whole Church gathers, thereby demonstrating its unity and community. But one could argue with far more justification that, in the context of the local denominational congregation, what happens on Sunday morning contributes to disunity rather than to unity.

The unchurched person is not bothered so much by the Church's insistence on confining worship to a single time and place. It is not a superhuman act, after all, to rise on Sunday morning. He is more alarmed by what the congregation would demand of him if he actually became involved. He contemplates the "activities" of the Church with something akin to the emotions of a skilled Cuban doctor who is told the only job available in the United States is that of janitor in the clinic. He will contribute to the maintenance of the building if something exciting is happening there, if what goes on jibes to some extent with his own sense of mission. Not finding this in the Church, he will seek out another community which offers him a chance to give of his talents. *What this suggests is a different principle of congregational organization, one that frees the layman to do what he does best, which calls him to involvement on the basis of mission as well as shared faith.*

When one considers the matter of taste, one finds considerable vehemence within the unchurched remnant. To many outsiders, the Church suggests bad music, hollow ritual, and sermons without content. Music is a particular stumbling block. The typical performance of many congregations strikes the outsider as a cross between rural nostalgia (lyrics) and television soap operas (melody). The majesties of Bach, Handel, and Mozart or the vitality of modern folk music and the Negro spiritual are missing in most congregations. Singing lacks spirit, and choirs tend to be mediocre. In most cases a stereophonic recording system would be a welcome alternative to the organ. Again, local churches might pool their vocal resources to produce one choir that would be available to the whole community. *We are left with the maxim that the organization that tries to do everything well may end up doing nothing well.*

One might forgive musical deficiencies if the typical sermon had more to commend itself. There has been much talk within the Church about the decline of preaching. The vapid topical sermons of the 1950s no longer suffice. One is almost audacious enough to suggest that the only lively preachers today are those who, in Paul's phrase, are not ashamed of the Gospel. But biblical preaching—preaching which does not rely on the personality of the preacher but on his submission to a discipline of study and involvement with the texts—is as rare as the water of life in a dry season.

Biblical preaching is not merely the use of a passage of Scripture as a platform for ministerial convictions. Biblical preaching is based on the recognition (a hard pill to swallow

in many liberal congregations) that the Bible is more in-
sightful than we are, more true to reality than our imagina-
tions are, more demanding than our consciences, and more
redemptive than our human assurances to one another.
Biblical preaching avoids the shallow humanism of many
Protestant pulpits without lapsing into a rigid, spiritualized
fundamentalism. Biblical preaching makes us see ourselves
in the mirror of the history of Israel which culminates in
the God-man Jesus Christ. It is objective preaching in the
sense that it transcends the preacher: the untalented speaker
(humanly speaking) who preaches biblically is ten times
more relevant than the talented speaker who rambles on
about life and death and even social justice apart from any
confrontation with the searing and often surprising texts of
the Old and New Testaments. I firmly believe that we are
entering a time when truly biblical preaching is possible,
when the realities of that preaching jump forward to grip
the hearer of the Word. As Harvey Cox has pointed out in
his book *The Secular City,* we shall find in the great proc-
lamations (and denunciations) of the Bible appropriate
analogies to our own apocalyptic era. What the outsider
misses in most preaching is not a feeling of being up-to-date
(he has his radio and TV and newspaper) but a sense that
the Church has anything relevant to say *about* what is happening today. And I submit that the way to this relevance
is through the Bible and not around it. The minister who
truly takes the imperative of biblical preaching to heart will
find that he cannot perform this ministry along with the
countless other jobs that he is called to do. And if the proposed structure in this book does nothing else, it at least
offers the possibility of freeing those called to preach to do so.

It has been observed by many that the context of the
sermon, which allows virtually no chance for response by
the laity, detracts from the force of contemporary preach-

ing. In some congregations there has been an attempt to remedy this defect by organizing discussions immediately following the service or during the week so that laymen and clergymen can engage in mutual reflection. This is certainly another antidote to the off-the-cuff sermonizing that is all too common today.

Again the outsider's criticism suggests a positive proposal. *The Church ought to differentiate the tasks of the ministry so that persons responsible for preaching will have time to explore and discover appropriate means of proclamation in our time.* This differentiation can occur only if there is a restructuring of the Church at the local level.

Another affront to the outsider is the apparent lack of attention that is paid to the order of worship in church services. Many services have no discernible progression. There is little coordination of music, prayers, and hymns and virtually no congregational participation. Holy Communion is prefaced by Boy Scout recognition ceremonies and followed by an announcement that was forgotten earlier in the service. The existence of only one weekly service in most local congregations tends to produce an all-purpose affair devoid of significant liturgy and seemingly intent on being an ecclesiastical mulligan stew. There are, within the Protestant tradition, ample precedents for a variety of worship services. There is the profoundly moving Friends Meeting where silence is the rule. There is worship which permits a high degree of congregational involvement. The Episcopal liturgy, with its moving cadences, is surely appealing to many beyond the confines of the Episcopal Church. *Again what is needed is a structure that will provide Protestants with a variety of worship forms, from the silent practice of prayer to the preaching service to the Lord's Supper.* Ultimately, worship must be objective. That is, it must point beyond those gathered for worship and beyond the personalities of those conducting the service. If Protestant worship were to regain this objective character, congregations would have less reason to be defensive about the complaints of the outsider.

3

The arguments for positive change within Protestantism are strengthened by considering briefly the situation of four primary groups *within* the Church: the theological seminaries, the college chaplains, the clergy, and the laity. We shall find that each of these groups has a creative contribution to make to a total renewal movement. And we shall find, too, that each group is hampered by the current organization of the Church.

No institutions are better placed for a concerted attack on the problems of the Church than the theological seminaries. Denominational seminaries could abbreviate their glowing annual reports to make room for an appeal that the churches become sufficiently well-defined to give meaning and direction to seminary training. The great ecumenical seminaries —Yale, Harvard, Chicago, Union—could take the lead in charting the broad implications of Protestant renewal. Too often, when one suggests that such responsibilities should fall to the seminaries, one encounters extreme reluctance. As with the denominations, there is a preoccupation with self-preservation at work which blinds many seminaries to the disenchantment that already exists within their own walls.

A hypothetical example may illuminate the situation: Suppose that the Acme Training School was set up to meet a public demand for well-made oboes. For years, graduates turned out the most melodic oboes within memory. But times changed. The oboe market began to insist on little innovations—a new stop here, an extra bit of chrome there—until the specifications of the market were increasingly hard to meet. The oboe makers started to complain that they were being forced to provide a homogenized instrument that could do a bit of everything, but nothing well. "But the customer is always right," said the President of the Acme Training School. It never entered his mind to suggest that the customers were making impossible demands.

Seminaries once trained men to teach and to preach the Gospel. Today the seminary is asked to produce Jacks-of-all-trades, men and women who can preach, teach, administer buildings, run recreational programs, be diplomats, prophesy, and keep accounts. And the seminary responds by attempting to produce homogenized oboes. It passively fills the demands of the market (the local churches), rarely willing to accept the possibility that the market is itself out of kilter. Is there nothing to be learned from the fact that fewer and fewer seminary students intend to enter the ministry?

Today's seminary student is uncertain about the Church. He wonders whether the Peace Corps or some other direct-action vocation might not be preferable to life as a minister. The Church seems too often peripheral, interfering for the sake of its own survival. In another mood, he may ask himself what things would be like if the job description of the clergyman were rewritten to enable him to do what interests him—to explore, on a full-time basis with the church membership, the implications of the Christian faith. How many congregations, he asks, would accept *that* definition of the minister?

He attends seminary for three years, pondering such questions. Then, quite suddenly it seems, the time comes to decide—about ordination, about what job to take, and he compromises more often than not, secure only because he knows others are sharing the same agony. He bows half-heartedly to the prevailing forms of the Church and weakly espouses a clerical image in which he no longer believes. Hell, for him, becomes not the absence of God's grace, but possibly the self-chastisement that takes place when the compromise is exposed. Perhaps it is the absence of a clear goal beyond seminary that leads to impatience about community, worship, and life in general that sometimes seems to pervade his life as a student.

Then, too, the seminary experience helps to create a chasm that will grow, if one is not careful, between the minister and the layman. In the process of learning theology, the student picks up what can only be described as a professional jargon, a sort of shorthand that enables him to communicate with his colleagues but not with humanity as a whole.

Until fairly recently, many seminaries have been out of touch with, or uninterested in, the practical problems facing the Church. One thinks of Reinhold Niebuhr and the late Paul Tillich. While Niebuhr may speak compellingly of sin, grace, man, and history, his concern with the Protestant Church *per se* has been negligible. Niebuhr has been essentially a great Christian apologist totally outside the context of the institutional concerns of the Church. Tillich, too, displayed scant attention to the problems of Protestantism as an institution, though it must be acknowledged that both he and Niebuhr were unstinting in their generosity to various church groups.

The typical curriculum within the modern seminary suggests a double standard in relation to the institutional Church. There are generally two areas of study, the academic (theology, Bible, Church history), and the so-called "practical field." Almost all discussion of the problems facing contemporary Protestantism are dealt with only in the "practical" courses. In the intellectual aura of the seminary these courses are regarded implicitly, if not openly, as somewhat second-rate. Likewise, there is a tendency to regard teachers in the practical field as second-class academic citizens. Fortunately, this gap between practical and academic concern is beginning to narrow, to the mutual benefit of both fields. Specialists in practical areas such as missions, preaching, Christian education, and ethics seem to be gaining more stature on seminary campuses. And a number of professors in the traditionally academic areas are turning their attention to the Protestant malaise. One thinks of Johannes Hoekendijk, Martin Marty, Franklin Littell, Langdon Gilkey, Robert Lynn, and Harvey Cox, among others. Hopefully we are passing from an age of abstraction to one of practical concern within the seminaries. But the official silence generally remains. The seminaries have yet to state their case for a renewed Protestantism. They have hesitated to alter their own programs and question their own goals.

In the context of this present impasse there is at least one thing that students can do and, indeed, are doing. That is to recognize that their major preparation for the ministry may take place outside of the formal classroom setting. If substantial numbers of students rally to something like the proposals in this book, for example, there is no reason why they should not set up their own discussion groups, calling on interested faculty members to provide insight at various points. Such a strategy would create some pressure on existing administrative mores, but at the same time it would have the constructive possibility of truly aiding the development of a student strategy for renewal. Organized seminary students could begin to insist, for example, that ordination as presently practiced by the denominations be viewed in the searing light of St. Paul's definition of the Body of

Christ in I Corinthians 12 and Romans 12. Students have begun to play a constructive role on the university campus by dramatizing certain weaknesses of secular education. There is no reason why theological students could not do the same on seminary campuses.

The continued isolation of the seminary from the Church-at-large would constitute a major stumbling block to renewal. In fact, a restructured seminary emerges as a basic ingredient of an over-all strategy for a more relevant Protestantism. The seminary of the future will have to take lay training as seriously as ministerial training; it will have to decentralize faculty to meet pressing needs beyond its own walls; it may have to support new styles of ministry as demonstration projects to the Church-at-large. In many cases, seminaries may be called on to play an integral part in the renewal of the Church in the immediate areas where they are located. Whatever the changes, the present unrest in Protestant seminaries must be directed to constructive action.

4

A second force within Protestantism is located on college and university campuses throughout the nation. College and university chaplains include within their ranks some of the most vocal and talented representatives of the ministry. They have provided responsible leadership in the civil rights movement; they have been able in many cases to interpret the restless and hopeful spirit of the new student generation; and they have played a crucial role in the important task of making the Christian faith intelligible to today's burgeoning student population. In addition, along with professors of religion in secular schools, chaplains have been among the most able recruiters of high-caliber students for the seminaries. And yet, as with the seminaries, there exists a deep chasm between the life of campus Christian groups and the Church-at-large. The most talented chaplains often play down the Church, characterizing it as an institution that has little to do with true Christianity. Indeed, student rebellion against conventional religion is often the "in" the chaplain needs to assert that Christianity is something more than a succession of bazaars, rummage sales, superficial sermons, and irrelevant social pronouncements. For this reason the chaplains are sometimes criticized as mavericks whose appeal to students varies with their willingness to "knock" the Church.

But this is unjust. Precisely what the churches need is a maverick spirit which is, at the same time, concerned with the potential effectiveness of the Church as a total institution. Unless there is a relevant Church structure into which college and university graduates can move, the best chaplains will be involved in nurturing momentary enthusiasm and unrealistic expectations. But these chaplains are in a position to tell the Church-at-large that rising educational levels call for a comparably higher level of intellectual, theological, and social awareness in the Church if it is to attract the coming generations. They could encourage students to use the corporate power they possess to demand specific changes in Church structure.

There are obvious problems involved. One would not expect the assembled college chaplains of America to inform the seminaries of their unwillingness to encourage students to enter the ministry until there is a substantial change in the way that this vocation is defined. Nor is it likely that chaplains will contribute to the debate on Church renewal unless they are asked to do so. And, to be sure, there are chaplains who scarcely fit into the mold suggested above, who are more interested in pushing parochial denominational programs on campus than in pressing for ecumenical structures of mission and service. Nevertheless, it is worth emphasizing that if the most able chaplains do not begin to concern themselves with the renewal of the Church as a whole, they will find themselves in the frustrating position of encouraging a revolution that has no chance of realization beyond the confines of the campus.

5

Within the ordained Protestant ministry, whether in the offices of the denominations or the parsonages of local churches, there is also considerable unrest. One of the most common topics of conversation among clergymen today deals with leaving the ministry. There is great dissatisfaction with the present job definition of the clergyman. And one finds increasing frustration among ministers of all ages at the apparent unwillingness of laymen in their churches to move away from traditional patterns of activity. One Presbyterian urban executive, Richard Moore, summed up his restlessness in the following words:

The member of the church who is concerned about important issues, and there are many such members, may find more in common with practicing pagans than with the nice folks who assemble in the church basement for that pot-luck dinner followed by a magic show, a "how-to-do-it" film on bowling, and a Disney cartoon for the kiddies. The sizzling issues of a mass society confront us in the business office, on the picket line, at the planning commission. Conversation in church parlor and kitchen is often no more than gossip flavored with pious platitudes. An officer of a local women's association told me . . . , "The way to involve women in the church is to get their hands in

dishwater up to the elbow." Here is an honest apostle for the
kind of church busywork that is too much with us. Dishpan
evangelism is only an exaggerated symbol of our disengagement.*

Edward Heininger, a minister involved in forming a new
congregation, expressed a common sense of discouragement
at the preoccupation of many local congregations with maintaining traditional images of ecclesiastical "success":

Although most churches begin in temporary quarters, the ex-
pectation is that a building will be constructed as soon as possible. . . . The property which was purchased for our church has
on it a large, three story brick house which we remodeled to
provide worship and educational facilities. . . . But even our
Church House did not fit our congregation's expectations. "People
will not come to this house because it does not look like a church,"
they say, although they come themselves.**

This preoccupation with buildings is only one aspect of
ministerial discouragement with the status quo. "The only
reason I go to church," writes the Rev. Donald Keating, "is
because I am a minister, because only the minister, in many
cases, has a ministry. He ministers to the sick, the dying, and
the mourners. He ministers through preaching and counseling. When the minister becomes the only one with a
ministry, it is a sick, sick church. . . . Unless the total
congregation participates in the task of ministering, the
true task of the ordained minister becomes impossible."

Here is the clue to a major stumbling block to the renewal
of the Church—the tragic failure of Protestantism to clearly
define and implement a working relationship between the
ministry and the laity. Traditionally the minister has been
a resource to the laity, providing him with the understand-

* *Renewal,* March 1964.
** *Renewal,* March 1963.

ings he needs to realize his Christian faith in the market place. But today's ministers, at least many of them, seem so discouraged with the social irrelevance of the Church that they have added to their already crowded schedule the task of doing what the layman ought to do. It is the ministers, primarily, who have represented the churches in the civil rights struggle, who have fought for justice in the metropolis, who have assumed the prophetic mantle that ought to fall on the shoulders of the Church membership. There is little question that this clerical activity has helped wake the Church up. But the time has come to re-evaluate this strategy in terms of the infinitely greater potential of the laity for constructive witness in the world.

If unrest among the clergy cannot be channeled into a constructive renewal movement, the chances are it will continue to grow with little hope of attaining anything but a further decline in the number of men and women who elect to enter the ministry. But consider the alternative: the organization of ministers across denominational lines to fight for a truly ecumenical Church structure; the joint action of committed clergymen to insist on certain standards that must inform the life of the Christian community; and, finally, sufficient redefinition of the ministry itself to make it an authentic vocation rather than a center of isolation and frustration.

6

The greatest potential force in the Church is the laity. It is also the most misused.

To be sure, there has been much discussion in recent years of "the role of the laity." But it is mostly ministers who have done the talking. For a number of reasons, including many of those outlined earlier in this chapter, the layman has either refused or been shielded from the task of exercising a progressive voice within the Church. Unquestionably there exists within the laity an element of strong conservatism, whether expressed in "dishpan evangelism" or in the refusal of some Church members to support denominational stands on race. The structure of the Church probably gives this element a power beyond its actual numerical strength. For one thing, the governing boards of the Church —trustees, councils, vestries, consistories—tend to be made up of the more conservative Church members. Their competence in financial affairs and prestige in the community at large seems to be as great a factor in their selection, as is their sense of mission. In the fall of 1964 *The Episcopalian* magazine included a profile of lay representatives to the Church's General Convention. With evident pride, the magazine told the deputies-to-be:

At least twenty-four of you are financial managers; twenty, industrial managers; fourteen, general managers; and three, institutional managers. . . . Among your numbers are more than fifty lawyers. . . . You include one or more of the following: dentist, designer, natural scientist, social worker, teacher, and private school dean. You also include at least ten insurance agents, seven advertising salesmen, four real estate agents, and four farmers. Young people in your midst are rare; and at least five of you are retired. . . . Most of you will be paying the major portion of your own expenses.

The pattern is repeated in other denominations, even though the membership of the Church embraces a far wider social and economic range. The Church might take a leaf from the War on Poverty legislation that states that all programs should be "developed, conducted, and administered with maximum feasible participation of residents of the areas and members of the groups served."

Younger laymen—and within Protestantism this can mean persons up to, and through, the age of forty—have a limited official voice. And as *The Episcopalian* profile shows, when election to major Church conventions is involved, it helps to be a vice-president with cash. One might argue that this pattern exists only in the larger congregations, particularly in suburbia. But how many small congregations, especially those in the inner city, are given a voice in the major forums of the Church?

Even if Church conventions were more representative, it is questionable whether the laity could inaugurate serious reforms. The sad reality is that laymen are rarely given an opportunity to vote on substantive issues of Church policy and programming. This is because these issues are rarely raised in specific form. Questions of membership standards, major changes in financial policy, or alteration of forms of Church government are seldom brought up, much less brought to a vote. The layman's role in denominational decision-making is most often limited to the ratification of matters that have already been predetermined by the Church bureaucracy. Even if a layman takes a progressive stand within a particular denominational board, his decisions can be offset by another countervailing wing of the denominational establishment. Perhaps it was this sense of frustration that led Thomas Ayers, President of Commonwealth Edison Company, to tell the assembled delegates to the General Synod of the United Church of Christ in 1965:

Many times the laymen have been way ahead of the clergy. We have found that constructive conflict is a good thing. And we have found that there is much less risk in change than in not changing.

[We ought to] call upon a management consulting firm . . . to render a report on what forms will give our church the greatest effectiveness. . . . [This] would be especially fruitful at our national level, where a welter of semi-autonomous instrumentalities, councils, and commissions exists. As a businessman, I must say that the top structure of our church looks cumbersome and inefficient. To me it is not sufficient that it works or that it is a comfortable compromise. The real question is whether it is the best we can devise to serve today's world.

One wonders, though, whether management consulting firms are more than a partial answer. A Lutheran group hired the services of one such firm and ended up evaluating its work in terms of the rather frightening notion of "Gross Synodical Output." Obviously, there is need to settle on the functions of the Church before becoming immersed in the problems of efficiency.

Nonetheless, there are many laymen who are discontented with the business-as-usual atmosphere of much Church life. Ministers' complaints about the laity are often a weak excuse for ministerial failure to educate their congregations to the demands of Christian discipleship. The desire of the laity to assume their proper role is indicated in part by the vigorous response of considerable numbers of Church members to experimental ministries outside the context of the local congregation. Among such ministries are:

The Chicago Business Industrial Project, which offers laymen a chance to reflect on the ethical dimensions of work in the modern metropolis.

Kirkridge and Parishfield, two retreat and study centers in

Pennsylvania and Michigan respectively, which provide a wide variety of seminars on basic issues facing the Church and the metropolis.

The Blue Hill Center outside of Boston, which has stimulated lay involvement in the civil rights movement.

The Volunteer Training Program of the Chicago City Missionary Society which trains laymen in specific areas of involvement in the inner city.

The Ecumenical Institute, also in Chicago, which provides intensive study courses for laymen.

These are only a few of many possible examples, but they all suggest a common pattern. These experimental ministries are specialized in what they do; they are ecumenical; they relate to churches within a given geographical area; and they are participation-oriented. Their primary focus is on preparing the laity for a ministry in the world. A new structure for Protestantism would make such patterns the rule rather than the exception.

Perhaps one of the reasons why lay involvement has been so sporadic is that we have failed to recognize that the most creative laymen are presently (in many cases) on the fringes of today's local congregations. They are on the periphery, and their hesitation in becoming involved with present activities is not so much an expression of apathy as of disinterest in today's status quo. But fully as important are the numbers of lay people who are immersed in the institution and who feel, quite wrongly, that there is nothing they can do. There is! Once the laity realizes that it is within their power as trustees, officers, and voting members to work at the grass roots for constructive, ecumenical renewal, once the laity realizes that there is no other force in the Church that can truly do this job, once the laity sees the possibilities for action inherent in the cooperative-ministry approach which we shall outline—once these things occur, the tide of irrelevance may turn, and a truly exciting movement may develop.

Even if there were no unrest within the seminaries, on the campuses, among both the ministry and the laity, even if the outsider's case against church attendance is discounted, the imperative for Protestant renewal would remain. For in the final analysis the Church must be obedient not to human desires but to the Gospel of Jesus Christ.

Chapter 4
The Theological Basis
for Renewal

1

Is there something to be said to men, that only a Church can say? I believe so, though in this age the saying cannot be too final or comprehensive. In St. Paul's phrase, "We see through a glass darkly."

We can say to one another and to mankind that there is a distinctly biblical understanding, capable of becoming Christian faith, that differs from other religious understandings, and casts important light on secular creeds and ideologies.

We can say that there is one God whose presence is manifest, not because we wish Him into existence, but because we know Him to be active. We can say that the world and history continue because of Him, for we know that man is incapable of living without an often hidden but nonetheless discernible grace.

We can say that man's nature is both good and evil, that man is both slave and free, weak and strong. We can say

51

that there is no division between body and spirit, as the Greeks thought, but that man is a unity: his responsibility cannot be evaded by positing a transient evil (the body) and an untarnished good (the soul).

We can say that Christ reveals God, in suffering love, in paradoxical parables, in crucifixion and resurrection. We can say, too, that the Bible is inspired, not because it was literally written by God, but because it records the mark of God upon the world, the story of the advent of Jesus Christ and the reactions of witnesses.

We can say that this Book points to affirmation in the face of all that would lead us to denial.

We can say that the faith we have is most often the result of intense seeking, of shattering crisis, of guilt exposed and forgiven, of a sojourn in the wilderness. And we can hope that our knowledge of the Gospel sometimes becomes incarnate in our lives—in anger at injustice, in a capacity to love, in a sporadic joy that perceives majesty in mystery.

We can reject the notion that God does things for us in the crass sense of positive thinking. Faith in Him, His Son, and His Spirit does not confer magical protection against the tragedies of life; it does not make one "better" than those outside. But we can say that at certain moments our vision of reality is transformed; our apprehension of Hell is overpowered by a sense of Heaven. And we can say that there are those who have been given the strength to live—literally, to overcome the temptation to suicide—because of this transformed vision.

And we can add what strikes many as the greatest superstition—that the sacramental audacity of the Church, in baptism and Holy Communion especially, is for one with a transformed vision a sharing in a vast, magnificent victory whose sign is suffering, not the suffering of man and the world primarily, but of an agonized Christ who takes the sin and weakness of the world upon Himself and emerges Victor.

Why, then, the Church? Because the Church says such things and occasionally embodies them. Always in the world somewhere the affirmations are made sufficiently manifest to create a suspicion of truth.

It is this sense that leads one to say that the Church exists to proclaim the Gospel, to preach, to teach, to share the sacraments, and to witness to Jesus Christ in the world. And with that there can be no equivocation or quarrel.

2

But there is always a sense in which theology—one's response to the revelation of God—tends toward a justification of human pretensions rather than the clarification of divine reality. Thus, while it might be possible to write a stronger theological brief for the Church structure proposed in this book, I am hesitant to do so. One could cite the Old Testament prophets and the sayings attributed to Christ and provide a rather overwhelming argument that the Church's first task is to love humanity rather than to insist on a particular phrasing of doctrines and beliefs. One could isolate a specific theological insight, such as justification by faith, and tailor the Church to the particular doctrine in question. But I suspect that such an effort would weaken the case. It is one thing to have a vision of God. It is another thing to tailor that vision to a specific social order. God is somehow more than a co-worker with man who can be summoned to place an imprimatur on human plans. Biblical truth is too wide and paradoxical—and, at times, absurd —to yield easily to the ABC's of ecclesiastical programming.

Indeed, my basic feeling is that a united and coordinated

mission on the Church's part is more essential than a theology which is universally accepted in every detail. One hesitates to make Dostoevsky's radical sense of freedom a casualty of St. Augustine's near determinism. One is reluctant to reject all of Karl Barth because he disagrees at certain points with Reinhold Niebuhr, or all of Niebuhr because he disagrees with Barth. If we were to edit the Bible on the basis of strict theological consensus, we might be forced to eliminate half the New Testament and five or six books of the Old Testament. If every profound theological insight had to be strained through the routinized colander of a fixed ecumenical theology, the result would be meaningless because it would lack depth and complexity. Thus while I would argue that an ecumenical renewal movement might use as basic statements the Apostles' Creed and "The Basis of the World Council of Churches," as stated at New Delhi in 1961, there is no reason why a renewed Protestantism might not allow for divergent interpretations of the Gospel within its fellowship. Within certain limits, such diversity would not be a cause of impotence. We have seen theology made an excuse for institutional self-interest too often to trust those who hide in its shadow, refusing to move in any positive direction.

Perhaps the greatest argument against this book's proposal is that the best way to guarantee theological diversity is to maintain the present denominations of Protestantism in their present form. Then, the argument might go, we would all be free to respond to biblical realities in our own several ways. Let one point be very clear. The proposal of this book is not aimed at eliminating this denominational diversity. *It is aimed at restoring it.* What we now have is not diversity but endless repetition based largely on the competition of the various denominational congregations for membership. Denominational worship services tend to be indistinguishable one from the other. This book proposes that the insights of the denominations be hammered out in the context of true dialogue and sharing at the local level. Today one must join an individual denominational congregation. In the renewed structure one would learn that true community is not the bland acceptance of a bland series of bland propositions, but the coming together of various positions which derive strength from existing side by side in a dialogue situation. We have today what is called public worship in most congregations. But it is not really public; it is private, and, because there is almost no free exchange of insight and conviction, it tends also to be static and stagnant. It can be predicted with some assurance that if the present denominational pattern continues, we shall have not diversity but a banal uniformity based more on a common dedication to self-preservation than a common quest for truth and community.

What is needed, in my opinion, is what might best be called a "working theology." Such a theology accepts fully the necessity for continued scholarly appraisal of the sources of Christian tradition, the Bible in particular. It champions the claims of religious freedom, the right of any man to profess his beliefs without provoking persecution by the Church or the State. It combines optimism and pessimism. Insofar as it is optimistic it stresses the freedom and the responsibility of man to work toward the building of a tolerable life on this earth, a society which provides a maximum of peace, justice, and liberty for every man. It is concerned both with the individual and with life in its corporate aspect. It accepts the goodness of the creation and the divine potential within man to master, insofar as possible, the environment in which he lives. It accepts the inherent potential of the secular city.

But this optimism is tempered by the very nature of the

biblical message and by the awful realities of our time: the specter of progress threatened by the demonic capacity for self-destruction that exists within the souls of men and nations, by the persistence of tragedy and the shadow of the bomb. We cannot take lightly the insights that produced the so-called "crisis theologies" of the first half of this century. We must recognize suffering, not simply as an ill to be attacked by changing the environment, but as a sign of the tragic nature of human destiny.

A working theology bases its faith, hope, and love not on the human capacity for embodying these attributes or on the magic of science or on the potential of any man-made government to ensure the world's ultimate safety. Faith, hope, and love are grounded, in the sense that the God who seems weak is truly strong, that the Spirit who seems fleeting is able to work miracles, that Christ whose resurrection we trust will be revealed as risen indeed. Faith, hope, and love are seen as leading to involvement in a world beyond this world, which stands in judgment over and against it. But at the same time we involve ourselves in the pains and joys of the present world.

3

Perhaps the most important theological fact of our time is that we are still here. The early Christians were convinced that the world was doomed, that the Judgment was at hand. But the world remains, doomed to ultimate extinction by natural causes quite apart from any eventual intervention from beyond. It is true that the Christ event as understood by the New Testament did not foreclose human history, but which of Christ's apostles imagined that the wicked world would last as long as it has?

The entrance of God into history in the person of the man Jesus, His crucifixion and resurrection, was an extraordinary revelation of the divine nature. It revealed for all time that the absolute nature of God is to forgive the man who repents and turns to Him. But it was not the End. It was not the completion of some celestial poker game in which the only remaining task was to gather in the chips in the form of souls won. No, God was and is still involved in history, and Christ is comprehensible as one whom we see through a glass darkly, sporadically, but not yet face to face, eternally. Christ lives as an indestructible aspect of God whose victory is forgone but not yet achieved.

There is still the suggestion of a God whose power is challenged in the arena of history by demonic forces—the Devil if you will—a power fundamentally opposed to the best in man and to the working out of God's will. The Devil is not the sum total of human evil. Man cannot so easily evade responsibility. The Devil is an objective reality. At times he seems the Absolute Enemy, a power who embodies all the forces of evil and is fully a match for God. At other times he seems a force for confusion, the price that God pays to allow man a measure of freedom, a haze that envelops a universe that ultimately is in God's hands. He may be, in the terms of the late Norbert Wiener, either a Manichaean Devil or an Augustinian Devil, but he exists nonetheless. Norman Mailer has illuminated the sense in which I speak of a Devil in his observations on the theological meaning of the slaughter of the Jews during World War Two:

. . . But if there is any urgency in God's intent, if we are not actors working out a play for our own salvation, but rather soldiers in an army which seeks to carry some noble conception of Being out across the stars, . . . then a portion of God's creative power was extinguished in the camps of extermination. If God is not all-powerful but existential, discovering the possibilities and limitations of His creative powers in the form of the history which is made by His creatures, then one must postulate an existential equal to God, an antagonist, the Devil, a principle of Evil whose signature was the concentration camps, whose joy is to waste substance, whose intent is to prevent God's conception of Being from reaching its mysterious goal. . . . It is not so comforting a postulation as the notion of God Omnipotent able to give us Eternal Rest, but it must also be seen that if God is all-powerful, the Jews cannot escape the bitter recognition that He considered one of His inscrutable purposes to be worth more than the lives of half His chosen people.*

The Church ought really to be the New Israel, meaning that it ought to be a people committed to the working out of God's purposes within history. The purpose is to serve, to evangelize by showing forth the struggle, not to form a nice little club that revels in benefits already won and takes refuge from the world in sanctuaries and personal testimonials. We live between partial victory and what we trust and hope will be total victory. The Christ event widened the struggle to include the Gentiles. It clarified the nature of the battle. But it did not relegate the God of the Old Testament to a far-off cloud, which is where far too many academic theologies have placed Him. We need to recover the spirit of the prophets of Israel, the concreteness of the Psalmists, the deep spiritual wrestling of the Patriarchs and Job. We need to recover the sense of the God who is active in history, contemporary, emotional, argumentative, cajoling, loving, thundering. Again, Norman Mailer speaks to the Protestants in a passage dealing with the Jews:

Yet if the Jews have a greatness, an irreducible greatness, I wonder if it is not to be found in the devil of their dialectic,

* *The Presidential Papers,* p. 193.

which places madness next to practicality, illumination side by side with duty, and arrogance in bed with humility. The Jews first saw God in the desert. . . . In the desert, man may flee before God, in terror of the apocalyptic voice of *His* lightning, *His* thunder; or, as dramatically, in a style that no Christian would ever attempt, man dares to speak directly to God, bargains with Him, upbraids Him, rises to scold Him, stares into God's eye like a proud, furious, stony-eyed child.*

God is not distant! He is present, restless, discontented with human sin, commiserating with the oppressed, fighting with man and the Devil.

God's victory is a matter of faith looking forward, not of absolute certainty looking backward.

One who would involve himself with the God who is revealed in Jesus Christ will be sensitive to the contemporary clash of good and evil in the real and present world.

The Church is related to God as Israel was related to Him in the Old Testament: called to serve, given a covenant with the Lord, and, under divine mandate, to do justice in the world.

4

But for too long the Church has acted as if the war were over, as if man were a pawn. At its worst the Church has outdone Israel in idolatry, inspiring the wrath of an Amos: "I hate, I despise your feasts. I take no delight in your solemn assemblies."

The Hebrews were less ingenious than we. They lacked adding machines. They were unfamiliar with the intricate logic of pensions, building funds, and job security. We have

* *Ibid.,* pp. 190-191.

learned to dedicate our primary energies to such important questions as which comes first, the sanctuary or the educational wing, the suave preacher or the go-go administrator, the leadership gifts campaign or the door-to-door appeal. We send ministers out, not to preach the Gospel, but to insure the financial success of a foundering new Church development project.

So it is not Christianity that is irrelevant but its institutional expression, the Church, mired in its moralism and ceaselessly contemplating everything but the One who calls it into being. Popular religion has invaded the Church, but there can be no correlation between popular religion and Christian faith. The most hopeful sign today is that popular religion—the bane of Protestantism in the 1950s—seems to be losing popularity. The poor are growing too wise to buy it, and the rest of the population is becoming too sophisticated to need the pious nostrums that too many congregations provide.

The bulwarks of popular religion within Protestantism are moralism, cheap grace, and institutionalism. Moralism is a handy means of evading the pressing issues, the root problems, the deep sufferings of the world. If we can limit Christian obedience to the spheres of temperance, sexual prudery, and being a "nice guy"—a sort of don't-rock-the-boat, individual ethic that will assuage the middle-class conscience—then we shall have a stable Church and, after all, the work of the Church is God's work.

Or is it? The Old Testament suggests that God bypassed the safe sanctuaries of Israel to accomplish His sweeping purposes. During the Middle Ages, when Rome was more concerned with wealth than compassion, God produced St. Francis as a living judgment on the pretensions of the ecclesiastical establishment. Moralism has always been Protestantism's shield against risk and relevance. The Church becomes captive of the culture. But God works despite the nonsensical radio commercials that tell us we are out on a limb without Him, and advertise the Church as a sort of divine tranquilizer.

"Cheap grace"—Bonhoeffer's phrase—is pat-on-the-back Christianity that offers absolution in return for regular church attendance and generous outlays for the building fund. Cheap grace offers an aura of good fellowship as a shield against the possibility of the Divine presence. Cheap grace refers to the subtle process by which the Protestant is encouraged to perform good works, thus avoiding the disturbing possibilities of grace itself.

Then there is institutionalism, the failure to provide flexibility, the subordination of everything to survival. In Dostoevsky's Legend of the Grand Inquisitor, the Inquisitor asks Christ, "Why, then, art Thou come to hinder us? . . . Thou mayest indeed point with pride at those children of freedom, of free love, of free and splendid sacrifice for Thy name. But remember that they were only some thousands; and what of the rest?" This is the eternal question of institutionalism.

The Protestant version of Dostoevsky's Legend might be set in a denominational conference room. Christ would not be imprisoned, as in the Legend, but merely doubted. The Protestant counterpart of the Inquisitor would say: "Your notion, if you really *are* Christ, of human freedom may be followed by some in our Churches, but what of the rest— those who have never seen the vision or heard the Word? There will always be a remnant perhaps, but we must concern ourselves with the others, with those who need the activities, the services, yes, the comfort, that we provide. So leave us. We have budgets to plan, annual reports to write, statistics to gather. With luck, if there's not too much rocking the boat, we shall survive."

5

What, then, is the mission of the Church? The common answer of many who have spoken and written of the renewal of Protestantism is that the Church's mission is "to be in the world." Because this phrase has gained such wide currency it is important that we raise the question of what being "in the world" means.

For many partisans of Church renewal, the world is "where the action is." It is where the "big" decisions are made, where "history" is unfolding, whether before the TV cameras or behind the closed doors of the powerful. It is where the Church "ought to be," but most often is not. The distance between the Church and the world, so defined, is the distance between dishpan evangelism and the sizzling issues of the planning commission. To speak of being in the world, in this sense, is perhaps to lament the era in Western history when the Church was a temporal power. There is the haunting sense that the Church is no longer in the center of the stage. But there are few partisans of renewal who would advocate the seizure of political power as a solution to the problem of irrelevance. If the Church is to be in the world today, it will arrive not as master but as servant, minus the trappings of ecclesiastical authority.

Very often the "world" is much less glamorous than it seems to be. There is the perhaps subconscious tendency to feel that if we could just infiltrate Madison Avenue, General Motors, or even the White House, we would perforce be "in the world." But business, advertising, and politics can be more isolated and impotent than one might suspect. The very institution that seems crucial may prove peripheral in terms of its actual impact on events. History, as well as the making of it, is too complex to yield to easy generalizations about where power lies or who is the crucial decision maker. History often makes posthumous heroes of contemporary unknowns. The Montgomery Bus Boycott, which determined the future character of much of the civil rights movement, had its genesis when a courageous but certainly unprestigious Negro lady, Mrs. Rosa Parks, refused to give up her seat on a bus. Her refusal precipitated the modern nonviolent movement in the United States. A local minister, the Rev. Martin Luther King, Jr., emerged, following Mrs. Parks's decision, as a national leader. Who could have foreseen that a woman's stubbornness on a bus would be the locus of "the action"? This is not to deny that there are many visible power centers in our society that are in need of humanization and where the Church should be present. But there are times when we fail to consider that "the action" is much closer to home. We may run toward the world without seeing the world at our doorstep.

We shall err in our definition of the Church's mission if we see the world only as the stage on which the dramatic scenes of history are enacted. There is also the world of the constant, where change is slow and where pain and sorrow are unpublicized. The world changes, but it does not change. As a consequence the Church must be in the world as priest as well as prophet. If Christians support revolution without healing the wounds of both friend and enemy, they foster the illusion that social activism can overcome the conflicting truths of this life. So while the Church abandons itself to "the action," it must remember also the lonely, the hung up, the sick, and the dying. It is true that Christ said, "Let the dead bury their dead." But He also said, "Thy sins are forgiven thee. Rise up and walk."

St. Paul had ample opportunity to compare the drama of jail with the smaller dramas of weakness and pain, and he used the word "love" to describe the style of life needed both on the picket line and in the hospital corridor. It was not to be an insipid, never-angry, sentimental love. But it *was* to be a love that was aware of needs and sympathetic to human weakness. Without love, one could prophesy and be "nothing"—a clanging cymbal. The Church loves the world when it is oriented both to revolution and to constant, unglamorous needs. To be preoccupied with one and neglect the other is to lose balance: love then becomes not love but escape. But Paul also recognized that it was humanly impossible to combine revolutionary zeal and priestly concern within each individual. The Church was described by Paul as a Body whose several members performed different functions, all under the imperative of love. Protestantism has lost this sense of the Church. J. B. Phillips translates Paul's First Letter to the Corinthians 12:27-30 as follows:

Now you are together the Body of Christ, and individually you are members of Him. And in His Church God has appointed first some to be Special Messengers [Apostles], secondly, some to be preachers of the word, thirdly teachers. After them he has appointed workers of spiritual power, men with the gift of healing, helpers, organizers and those with the gift of speaking in "tongues."

As we look at the Body of Christ do we find that all are Special Messengers, all are preachers, or all teachers? Do we find all wielders of spiritual power, all able to heal, all able to speak with tongues, or all able to interpret the tongues? No, we find God's distribution of gifts is on the same principles of harmony that He has shown in the human body.*

Paul is speaking of specialization. He is recognizing that different persons are called to different tasks. The true unity of the Church is expressed in the term Body. Each function-

* J. B. Phillips, trans., *op cit.,* p. 58.

ing organ in the Body is essential to the life and unity of the whole. But one sees few such distinctions within the Protestant Church today. We lump most of the specific functions of which Paul speaks into the job description of the professional, ordained ministry. The laity emerges as the severed portion of an amputated body. The result is a Church which is neither priestly nor prophetic, a Church which cannot minister effectively in the world.

For in the last analysis it is obvious that the Church is inextricably in the world. It cannot escape. The Priest and the Levite were on the Jericho Road when the wounded man cried for help. The Church was in the world when the Inquisition was at the height of its power. The Church was also in the world when St. Francis spoke to animals and indigents. And it is in the world today—weak, divided, concerned and self-serving, helping and hindering, worshiping God and worshiping idols, but there nonetheless.

So the question is really *how* the Church is to be in the world. How is the Church—2000 years after the Christ event—to organize itself? The Bible provides ample cause for discouragement in the face of this question. At one level, the Scriptures can be seen as the story of man's abortive attempts to capture God, to freeze Him into an inflexible and easily handled mold. Man continually attempts to perform surgery on God—usually of the heart or brain—in order to avoid the passion of His restless activity in all the world and to escape the endless depths of His mysterious presence. But the Bible is also the story of God's response. He demonstrates the folly of these attempted operations in a supreme act of self-revelation culminating in the crucifixion of the God-man who consorted with prostitutes, cast out money-changers, and suggested the possibility of resurrection. He unleashes His Spirit in the world, and when man is seized by this Spirit he can no longer remain content with his little

efforts to confine God, to remove all the elements of risk
and joy and suffering that the Spirit opens up. Finally, one
must affirm that the Church that is deaf to the Spirit is not
the Church. And with that affirmation, one rests the case for
renewal, not on human plans and notions but upon the
biblical call for continued openness to the Will of God. If
our only achievement is to remove the cotton from the ears
of the Church, that Christians might stand ready to obey,
that is satisfaction enough.

Chapter 5
Proposal for a
Renewal Movement

1

In the first four chapters I have sketched some basic arguments for the development of an ecumenical renewal movement. I have suggested that such a movement would find positive response outside the churches; it would coordinate the existing natural groups within the Church; and it would move toward what can be called a working theology. Now it is time to develop the specific proposal for structural renewal suggested in Chapter One. We can begin by asking how the process of renewal might begin, assuming that the local congregation, in its present form, was maintained as the basic institution of Protestantism. First, one must consider the resources that are available.

Despite a needed emphasis on the importance of the laity, the crucial factor in the *initiation* of renewal is the minister of the congregation. If he lacks vision, if he is wedded to

67

traditional views, if he counts his success in terms of shiny new buildings and the ability to run a cozy social club, then the chances for renewal are irreparably damaged. It would be better if the congregation had no minister at all. For the first prerequisite of renewal is a minister who can lead the laity to see the need for a more relevant Church. The first, most positive step a congregation can take is to call the right minister.

It is rare to find a clergyman with all the qualifications a renewal-minded congregation has in mind. The congregation that wishes the minister to combine four or five specific skills, in addition to being outgoing and having an attractive but not too aggressive wife, is probably more interested in having a showpiece than a man who can point the way to the mission that lies beyond the sanctuary walls. Thus the local church would be best advised to choose a specific mission and seek out a minister who is able to devote his skills to a fairly specific area. The choice of mission is largely dependent on the nature and location of the particular congregation.

2

For purposes of discussion, we can point to three types of congregation that might fit into a pattern of renewed mission. The first type is the large, versatile congregation which is able to carry on more than one or two activities with a degree of competence. It has considerable resources, both financially and in terms of the talents of its membership. Such a congregation could carry out a teaching ministry of considerable scope and depth. It could perform some of the basic ministries of chaplaincy—public worship, preaching, and pastoral counseling.

The second type of congregation is smaller. It may have anywhere from several hundred members to virtually none. In terms of resources it could be designated as average. In order to have any mission at all, it must pick and choose. If such a congregation chooses to have a Sunday School for children and to support public worship, it is unlikely that it can do more than make a stab at other possible ministries. The primary possibility of renewal for such a congregation is to choose *one* mission and seek to perform it with all the skill and dedication of the combined membership. Several churches have done exactly this. They have curtailed excessive programming and concentrated on doing one thing well. But the process has been difficult, and certain factors have been present: a renewal-oriented minister and enough progressive lay leadership to overcome traditional objections. Only in the rarest instances have such congregations been able to perform the three functions outlined in the first chapter with any degree of completeness. If they have concentrated on chaplaincy or teaching, they have been forced to neglect abandonment. If they have chosen a specific area of abandonment (direct involvement in community affairs, for example), the chances are that chaplaincy and teaching have suffered.

The third type of congregation is the one that comes into being without laboring under the burden of past traditions. Such congregations are rare. They may sprout up as the result of a denominational "church extension" project, as when a minister forms a new congregation in an "unchurched" suburban area. Or they may be the result of a "reoccupation" of a local church whose old membership has moved or otherwise vacated the premises. Theoretically, such a congregation is free from the outset to determine the disciplines and mission that will guide their development. The members are bound by no rule save their sense of present obedience to the present will of God.

The only way to renew the first two types of congregation is through a long, arduous process of change—weeding out often-cherished organizations that no longer serve a justifiable purpose, developing adequate staff, training the laity, and choosing specific missions. The third type of congregation, while often following stereotyped patterns of development (lax membership requirements, emphasis on buildings rather than mission, etc.), provides the most striking examples of local Church renewal. The Church of the Saviour; the Aldersgate Methodist Church near Cleveland (whose development was recorded in Robert Raines's *New Life in the Church*); Judson Memorial Church in New York City, etc., were all developed within the last two decades practically from scratch. Judson Church, for example, had almost died out as a congregation when Howard Moody was called as minister in 1950. Moody recalls that the primary "spiritual asset" that the church possessed at that time was that "the corpse of the past was all but buried." There are lesser known examples of "starting from scratch." The Westover Hills Presbyterian Church, in Little Rock, Arkansas, limits its activities to a ministry of teaching. It now conducts one of the few truly exciting programs of adult lay education to be found in the American Church. The fact that a "traditional" ministry may have repercussions "in the world" is attested by the fact that Westover Hills laymen played a constructive role in mediating the Little Rock school crisis.

One is forced to the conclusion that renewal is most possible when the institutional life of the congregation is most flexible. Also, one can conclude that renewed local congregations that have started from scratch have tended to concentrate on specific mission functions, rather than on attempts to give equal emphasis to every function of the Church.[*]

3

But this scarcely solves the problem for the vast bulk of Protestantism, structured as it is around local churches that have existed for years and which do not yield easily to the idea of change. Ministers of such churches tend to be critical of renewal efforts precisely because they avoid the issue of ingrained, long-term resistance. It is in such churches that one finds the greatest sense of discouragement among the clergy. Are we to say that no significant change can take place within such congregations? Are clashes of personality too great in some? Is allegiance to tradition too strong in others? Do many of these churches simply lack the leadership, the talents, that might serve the cause of renewal? The answer is No, but it is a qualified No. For, in many cases the answer is Yes. Yes, there are potential clashes of personality that would develop into full-blown schisms if the cause of renewal were arduously pressed. There are, in many cases, such strong emotional ties to "the way we have always done things" that any but the most superficial changes in program or policy would result in chaos. What if First Church on Main Street were asked to give up its annual rummage sale on the grounds that it no longer represents what could be considered a valid Christian mission? What if St. John's by the Gas Station were asked to place a large sign in front of

[*] Reports on several attempts to renew local congregations can be found in *Who's Killing the Church?, A Renewal Reader,* 1966.

its building—WE SUPPORT AN END TO RACIAL DISCRIMINATION
IN HOUSING IN GREEN ACRES. If we are optimistic, if change
were proved possible, we would have to raise a second question. Could today's local church, assuming it wished to do
so, support within its own congregation the three functions
of the Church outlined in Chapter One?

Let us recall the three functions—chaplaincy, teaching,
and abandonment.

Chaplaincy suggests the priestly and pastoral ministry of
the Church. It is the aspect of the Church that deals with
preaching the Word of God, administering the sacraments,
pastoral counseling, and liturgy. Chaplaincy is primarily a
resource ministry to the laity. It is absolutely central to the
life of the Church. It recognizes St. Paul's assertion that some
are called to be preachers of the Word, some to be healers,
some administrators.

Then there is the ministry of teaching. To teach is to con-
vey in the most competent manner possible the central
themes of the Bible and to explore with the laity the nature
of the world into which Christians are called. Like chaplaincy, teaching is specialized.

The third function of the Church—abandonment—is implied in a key passage from Paul's Letter to the Philippians
(2:5-8), which J. B. Phillips translates as follows:

Let Christ Himself be your example as to what your attitude
should be. For He, Who had always been God by nature, did
not cling to His prerogatives as God's Equal, but stripped Himself of all privilege by consenting to be a slave by nature and
being born as mortal man. And, having become man, He
humbled Himself by living a life of utter obedience, even to the
extent of dying, *and the death He died was the death of a common criminal.*

* J. B. Phillips, trans., *op. cit.,* pp. 113-114.

This passage may be read, together with J. B. Phillips' translation of the famous words from Paul's First Letter to the Corinthians (13:4-8):

The love of which I speak is slow to lose patience—it looks for a way of being constructive. It is not possessive: it is neither anxious to impress nor does it cherish inflated ideas of its own importance.

Love . . . does not pursue selfish advantage. It is not touchy. It does not compile statistics of evil or gloat over the wickedness of other people. On the contrary, it is glad with all good men when Truth prevails.

Love knows no limit to its endurance, no end to its trust, no fading of its hope: it can outlast anything. It is, in fact, the one thing that still stands when all else has fallen.*

The Christian in the world must not "cling to his prerogatives." He must, the Church must, take the form of a servant. There must be abandonment to the imperatives of love —love that does not "pursue selfish advantage" or "compile statistics of evil." Our mind is to be that of Christ's, who emptied Himself of status, prestige, even life itself, for the sake of the world. The Church as chaplain and teacher is the resource that the laity needs if it is to abandon itself to the struggles of life in our time. The Church abandons itself when it takes the shape that the world needs. Such a Church will not shun the secular. It will seek to learn from the world a wisdom not available in sermons and sanctuaries alone. It will not be afraid to identify itself with forces in society that mirror the intentions of "all good men." The Church that abandons itself understands that prophecy without involvement is mere kibitzing. Abandonment is closer to parable than proclamation. It recognizes that the *actions* of Christ,

* *Ibid.*, pp. 58-59.

as much as His spoken words, were the crucial factors in
His ministry.

The Church that takes abandonment seriously will place
emphasis on experimental ministries, on participation in
direct action movements designed to bring about political,
economic, and racial justice, and on the mission of the laity
in the scientific laboratories, the legislative assemblies, the
centers of youth culture, the schools, and the wretched com-
partments where the aged are prematurely buried. It will be
concerned with the humanization of life where it is lived.

4

But who can honestly accuse the Church with being uninterested in chaplaincy, in teaching, in abandonment? Our
case here is that there are countless congregations who wish
to move forward, but who are so encumbered structurally
that movement is virtually impossible. And our argument is
that there is a structure that could provide at least the basis
for a ministry of chaplaincy, teaching, and abandonment.
The Church of the future will have to be built on a scale that
will provide all of its members with the resources of chaplaincy and teaching. Abandonment will have to become the
rule rather than the exception. In short, the local congregation, as we know it, will have to be radically transformed.

There are two possible approaches to the restructuring of
the local congregation. The first is the approach we have
already suggested—the gradual evolution of specific ministries in those local congregations structurally equipped to
move toward a posture of renewal. I tried at the outset of
this chapter to point out the limitations of such an approach,
the fact that even if an individual congregation takes seriously the ministries of teaching, chaplaincy, and abandon-

ment, *it is rarely in a position to implement all three functions.* Now I propose a second approach, no less difficult, but in the long run designed to produce a Church which *can* fulfill these functions. It is an approach that builds on the local, ecumenical cooperation of existing congregations.

Here, in my opinion, are the possibilities and advantages of what might be called the *cooperative ministry approach.*

Pastoral counseling would be provided in a given neighborhood in the name of the Church as a whole and not of individual congregations.

The teaching ministry of the Church would be performed on an around-the-week basis by trained teachers who could combine the resources of today's local congregations to provide educational resources for all age groups.

The preaching and worship ministries of the Church (chaplaincy) would pool the resources of local congregations in order to bring more diversity and depth to proclamation and worship and to provide a sufficient number of services to meet the spiritual needs of the total community.

Membership in a local congregation would be redefined in terms of commitment to specific missions of abandonment. Depending on the talents and interests of members of the Church, these specific involvements could be re-evaluated from time to time. Thus there would be two categories of Church membership—basic membership in the Body of Christ and specific membership in a working part of that Body.

The physical plants of existing local congregations would be administered centrally within a given area, and the use to which these buildings were put would be determined by the specific need for chaplaincy, teaching, and abandonment within the area.

Funds saved by the pooling of resources on the local level would be used to support experimental ministries and teaching projects designed to serve and involve the laity beyond the residential community.

Professional ministers and church workers would be selected on the basis of their ability to perform one of the specific ministries of chaplaincy, teaching, and abandonment.

5

Given a projected pattern such as this, what would become of loyalties to the local congregation as it is presently structured? A different sort of loyalty would develop. One would forfeit the "security" of knowing that the local church building is one's very own and that nobody from "outside" can change one jot or tittle of its familiar furnishings. The building would be given to the neighborhood, consecrated for specific mission activity. One's loyalty would be to the Church in action rather than the Church in repose. Within the cooperative ministry, loyalty would be to the whole Church embodied in the concrete realization of its various functions in a given area. The sense of community, of *koininia,* would emerge as one participated in the specific ministries of the Church. In a real sense loyalty would be to the world, because the abandonment ministries of the Church would necessarily involve members in the struggles and joys of everyday existence.

We have already suggested that the present structure of the Church tends to create a division between Church members and those outside, those who do not set foot on church property because they feel they will be pressed to join before they have a chance to learn what is happening, those who do not feel the Church offers an outlet for their talents. The cooperative ministry structure would be far more open. The public worship of the Church would not be the occasion for pressing the outsider to become a member. The ministries of abandonment would be open to the participation of all men. The evangelism of the Christian community would depend as much on the ministry of abandonment as on the ministries of teaching and chaplaincy. The ministries of abandonment would be living parables, raising the question within the outsider of what the Church is, of why it seems willing to give of itself without asking anything in return. He would be free to accept or reject, but at least the proposed structure would create the possibility of contact which scarcely exists today.

Lest one think we are perpetuating the activism that seems rampant within much of today's Protestantism, we should emphasize that neighborhood mission (involvement in the local, residential ministries of the Church) would be appropriate for some, but not for all. The fact is that such participation would be an escape for many church members. One thinks particularly of the suburban commuter whose basic responsibilities require involvement beyond the neighborhood where he lives. The present activism of the local church fails to recognize that one's job or one's involvement in broad secular associations is, for many laymen, the most appropriate area of mission. Laymen so involved *are* the Church, even as those who minister in the local neighborhood are the Church, even as those who support the traditional ministries of chaplaincy and teaching are the Church. Such laymen would be considerably more loyal to a church that demanded not institutional allegiance but allegiance to the imperatives of servanthood in the world. They would no longer feel that *their* work, *their* interests, and *their* complex decisions were something isolated from the Church's life. The new structure would provide for those who have no desire to be "active" in the traditional sense, and for those who do.

In an earlier chapter I suggested that decentralization is a positive step toward increasing communal involvement at the local level. Doesn't the idea of a cooperative ministry of several local congregations suggest centralization? Yes, but only to a certain extent. The fragmented ministries of today's local congregations would be brought together. As much as possible, the institutions of the Church would be cooperatively administered. Public worship would be an occasion when participants in the specialized ministries could gather in a single place. To this extent there would be centralization. But in terms of the current denominational framework of Protestantism, there would be a large degree of decentralization. No longer would policies of cooperation depend on the decisions of denominational offices far removed from the local scene. No longer would financial arrangements be predicated on the denominational system, by which funds are collected locally and used almost exclusively to perpetuate a pattern of denominational allegiance rather than allegiance to the Church as a whole. The proposed structure presupposes the necessity of decentralizing the denominations.

6

Perhaps the best way to describe the proposed structure is to suggest a hypothetical example of how it might work. If what follows seems overly concerned with finances it is because one of the major objections to a change in structure is that it would be financially impossible. Let us see.

Let us assume that ten churches in a given area decide to

pool their resources to form a cooperative ministry. Assume further that the average annual budget of these individual churches is $30,000 and that the average active membership is 250 adults. Taken together we would have an annual total budget of $300,000 per year and a total active membership of 2,500. In affluent suburbs, active membership and annual budgets would be more than double these hypothetical figures. In inner-city areas, both membership and financial resources might be reduced by as much as two-thirds. Our example can serve as an imaginary median between these two extremes.

Let us assume that one of the ten church buildings would serve as a center for the ministry of chaplaincy. Ideally it would be one of the larger facilities, with a seating capacity of 500 or more, and a small chapel that could be kept open all day, every day. This facility would serve as the center of a chaplaincy ministry to the total community. It would be a center of worship, preaching, and music. It would be a place where members of the specialized congregations could gather to reflect on the theological meaning of their involvements. We shall call this building the Central House. By *not* calling it a church we help to point to the fact that the church is not a building but a people, called to obedient response to the Gospel. The New Testament (Romans 16:5) makes reference to the "Church in the house" and it is a notion that could well be applied to the formal gathering place of the church. The Central House would have no formal programs beyond those connected with worship and the maintenance of a facility where the specialized congregations could gather. So we shall staff it with two full-time preacher-liturgists, a director of music, one secretary, and a maintenance man. If we average salaries out at $8,000 per year (well above the current ministerial average) and add $20,000 annually for light, heat, and repairs, we will require a total annual budget of $60,000. We shall assume that 100 of the 2,500 laymen feel called to volunteer their services to the ministries of the Central House, to help conduct services of worship, to assist in maintenance, ushering, etc., and to participate in a choir.

Three of the ten church buildings might be used to house the teaching ministries.

One could be specifically for the education of children. It would include a weekday nursery and a wide range of educational resources for children in the community. It would employ a full-time staff of two persons and a part-time maintenance man. In order to provide ample funds for salaries, maintenance, and program materials, we shall budget $30,000 a year. We shall assume that fifty laymen would volunteer to support this ministry with their time and talents.

A second teaching ministry would be aimed at the youth of the area. It would involve another fifty laymen, two full-time staff members, a half-time maintenance man, and another budget outlay of $30,000 a year.

The third teaching center would be concerned with adult lay education. We shall staff it with a single director and a secretary, but we shall give the director an ample budget so that he can afford to hire resource persons, train volunteer teachers, and experiment as necessary. So we shall budget another $30,000, including maintenance, and assume that another fifty laymen would volunteer, both as teachers and part-time staff members. The basic courses of these teaching centers would be supplemented with lectures, films, and other services to the community at large.

So far we have budgeted $150,000 and involved only 250 laymen as volunteers in the programs of the cooperative ministry. We have covered the basic ministries of chaplaincy and teaching. What remains to be done? I would argue that the only remaining permanent facility needed would be a building or a rented space to accommodate an administrator for the cooperative ministry and a pastoral counseling center. For this, we could assume a budget of $50,000 a year and the involvement of another 50 laymen.

We can summarize with a simple diagram:

	Lay Involvement	Budget	Facility
Chaplaincy	100 volunteers	$ 60,000	Central House
Administrative and Pastoral Counseling Center	50 volunteers	$ 50,000	Adapt church building or rent space
Teaching	150 volunteers	$ 90,000	Adapt three church buildings
Totals	300 volunteers	$200,000	Four or five church buildings

We began our hypothetical model with ten congregations, ten buildings, and a combined annual budget of $300,000. We assumed a total membership of 2,500 adults. At this point we have at least five remaining church buildings to do with as we choose, an extra $100,000 which we have not budgeted, and more than two thousand laymen who are as yet uninvolved. In other words we have flexibility.

Take first the five remaining buildings. We can sell them, if we choose, and use the proceeds to buy or rent facilities that are more appropriate for the ministries of abandonment. We can hire specialized professionals to serve as resource persons in the task of involving the laity in direct service ministries. We can use the unbudgeted income to support local community organization projects, city-wide specialized ministries, or less affluent cooperative ministries in other areas.

The remaining laymen would be recruited for the ministries of abandonment, although their involvement would depend on their analysis of their total commitment and whether this commitment lay primarily in the residential community. They would be encouraged, as at present, to participate in the worship life of the gathered community. They would be expected to avail themselves of the teaching resources of the Church.

This outline has necessarily been sketchy and hypothetical. A cooperative ministry could involve more than ten churches, or less. The amount of money needed to maintain buildings and pay salaries would vary. But we have said enough to suggest some of the basic principles involved: a differentiation of structure; a combining of resources so that chaplaincy, teaching, and abandonment can develop in a given neighborhood; and a redefinition of the local congregation in terms of basic membership and specific mission.

7

The cooperative ministry idea also suggests a means by which both the seminaries and the denominations could participate in a plan of renewal. Let us retain our hypothetical model for a moment.

So far we have spoken of what local churches might accomplish on their own initiative. Suppose, in addition, that a theological seminary were to enter the picture. The current practice of many seminaries is to encourage students to take an intern year—a year of practical field experience—prior to graduation. We shall assume that our hypothetical seminary has a direct relationship with our hypothetical cooperative ministry, so that a continual flow of intern-year students is available to work within the various specialized ministries. Because this would be seen as an integral part of theological education, the seminary would also supply one faculty member each year, not only to act as a resource to the students, but also to participate directly in one of the ministries. A professor of Old Testament, for example, could supplement the staff of the adult lay training center. A professor of Christian ethics could participate in a ministry of abandonment, possibly a lay task force devoted to changing unjust housing laws. In this way seminaries could provide students with supervised field experience, but, just as important, seminary faculties would be far less isolated from the Church-at-large.

We can carry the illustration even further. If six or eight students each year were affiliated with the cooperative ministry, would it not be just as possible to send six or eight laymen to the seminary for specialized training or basic theological education? If this could be achieved, the split between the seminary and the Church would be virtually nullified. The seminaries would be forced to make room in their midst for the layman, and the mere presence of the laity would be a protection against the abstraction that often diverts theology from the Church. Seminaries would be loath to enter such a program unless there were a cooperative ministry that could creatively use the talents of their students. Indeed I can see no way other than the one suggested to begin to solve the problem of the seminary's isolation.

How, then, might the denominations be involved? Let us imagine that the denominations saw, and accepted, the trend toward local cooperative ministries. They would be in a position either to encourage it or seek to prevent it. If we are exceedingly optimistic, we could expect support from at least some denominations. Suppose, for example, that four or five major denominations agreed to encourage a cooperative ministry movement. They could pool certain funds to support cooperative ministries in the initial phases of development. But they could do something even more helpful. They could decentralize their own denominational programs and offer them, on an ecumenical, no-strings-attached basis, to clusters of cooperative ministries. They could move talented staff members from central offices to positions within the cooperative ministries. They could help provide regional resources to support ministries of abandonment and teaching that could not be carried out locally.

There are other elements that might come into play to aid the development of a renewed Church structure. The organizational pattern of abandonment would enable local communities to form interfaith structures and not-for-profit groups that would have far more community effectiveness than any program sponsored by a single congregation or denomination would possess. Abandonment would also emphasize cooperation with secular service agencies, thus increasing ministry without adding to the maintenance of Church institutions. Since traditional church buildings would play a less important role than at present, there would also be a considerable reduction in capital expenditures. The edifice complex of modern Protestantism would be cured.

It may seem mundane to dwell on finances, but there is one other question that must be faced. Would there not be an inevitable decrease in giving among members who do not accept the cooperative ministry concept? Consider first the current levels of giving to the Church as it is presently structured. In 1961, according to the *Yearbook of American Churches,* thirty-nine Protestant and Eastern Orthodox denominations received contributions totaling just over two and one-half billion dollars. Eighteen per cent of this amount was designated for "benevolences"—a term that applies to all expenses beyond the maintenance and programs of local congregations. Local expenses, in ministers' salaries, maintenance costs, etc., averaged $54.00 per member. The average per capita contribution for "benevolences" was just over $12.00. The per member annual contributions within the denominations involved in the Blake-Pike conversations on Church union average approximately $75.00. So the current level of giving within the Church is by no means extraordinary.

I would suggest that the renewed Protestant Church would gain enough in dedication from an enlivened laity to offset losses in contributions from today's nominal members. I would suggest also that the cooperative ministry idea, if widely followed, would result in major reductions of operating expenses. The actual number of church buildings would be cut in half. The unification of presently duplicated programs at the local level would result in eventual savings, despite the fact that the level of services would be vastly increased. And, with widespread intensive training of the laity, jobs that are salaried positions at present could be filled by volunteer help or eliminated.

The cooperative ministry approach would also streamline the cumbersome and often offensive methods that are currently employed to raise money in the Church. Funds would be raised once each year in an annual appeal to the total membership. There would be no special offerings and no time-consuming money-raising events such as bazaars and bake sales.

8

If the cooperative ministry is seen as the basic unit of the ecumenical Church, what sort of polity, or form of government, might it adopt? How would cooperative ministries be related to one another? This is scarcely a subject that can be dealt with in detail, but it is possible to suggest a few broad principles that may prove useful. The basic question involved is that of authority in the Church. Three general interpretations of authority exist within Protestantism. The Free Church, or Congregational, tradition invests complete authority with the local congregation. The minister is a member of the congregation; the congregation is free to develop its own rules of government. In general, final decisions rest on a democratic vote of the entire membership.

The second tradition is found within the Reformed or Presbyterian branch of Protestantism. Here one finds not the pure democracy of the Free Church but a representative system with certain rights reserved for the minister. It is not within the power of a local congregation, for example, to fire a clergyman because it disagrees with his sermons. There is also a line of authority extending from the local congregation to the Presbytery (made up of ministers and lay representatives of local congregations) to the Synod (made up of representatives elected by the Presbyteries) to the General Assembly, a national body of ministers and laymen which meets once a year and is the highest court of appeal. It is rather like the local, state, and federal system which is the basis of American politics.

The third basic form of government is Episcopal. It makes a basic distinction between the ordained ministry and the laity, although the layman does not lack power in terms of the actual functioning of the Church government. The Church is divided into districts, or dioceses, each presided over by a bishop who has (depending on whether he is Methodist or Episcopalian) varying degrees of power. In general the bishop can permit the formulation or dissolution of congregations, determine the ministers of local congregations, and, jointly with other bishops, exert considerable in-

fluence over the life of the total denomination. The basic
rationale behind the Episcopal form is the belief that the
clergy—and bishops in particular—are part of an Apostolic
Succession extending back through Church history to the
time of Christ.

It is my conviction that each of these three forms of government has elements that should be included in the polity
of a renewed Protestantism.

The Congregational system points to the need for local
self-determination in response to the will of God as it is
perceived at a given time and place.

The Presbyterian system provides checks and balances
which are needed to insure that no part of the Body of Christ
exerts disproportionate power.

Whether or not one accepts Apostolic Succession as literal
historical truth, the Episcopal system recognizes that the
ordained minister, through no virtue of his own, is the one
to whom the liturgical, sacramental ministry of the Church
is entrusted. Bishops, again through no inherent personal
virtue, are the spiritual leaders of the Church.

But how incongruous these forms are within the present
fragmented sea of Protestantism! Since none is generally
accepted, the independent validity of all is in question. *A
decision is called for and the most sensible decision is one
that takes from each system what seems most relevant to a
truly ecumenical Church.*

Among the three forms of government the Presbyterian
tradition represents what might be called the "middle road."
But there is no reason why the renewed Church could not
provide a measure of unassailable autonomy at the local
level. Nor is there reason to reject bishops in the context of a
Presbyterian system. At present, in terms of the actual power
structures that exist from denomination to denomination,

there is little discernible difference in the way that power is used or in the results of the use of power. Generally speaking, most local congregations hire (or fire) their ministers, regardless of the formal structure of the denomination they happen to belong to.

Most denominations fight over the same issues—especially in statements on racial justice—and most reach similar conclusions. Behind every form of government in modern Protestantism there is a denominational bureaucracy and, beyond the local congregation, regardless of what the form of government is, that is where the power lies.

9

The cooperative ministry, as I see it, is really a radical reinterpretation of the local congregation for our time. It recognizes the basic difficulties involved in fulfilling the demands of chaplaincy, teaching, and abandonment within the local congregation as it is presently defined. To be consistent, I would have to admit that, in some cases, these three functions *could* be fulfilled by *some* present-day congregations. But these are exceptions which merely tend to illuminate the prevalent disjointedness of Protestantism. Therefore we must reinterpret the local congregation in terms of the organization of clusters of present-day congregations to form a neighborhood Church. This neighborhood Church would include in its membership all present local congregations that, on the basis of their present polity, elected to become part of the cooperative ministry. For the time being, pending the possible unification of the national denominations, the cooperative ministry would determine its own mode of government on the basis of a decision of the total

membership. Such a government could include the following elements:

A recognition of chaplaincy, teaching, and abandonment as
three complementary aspects of the total ministry of the Church.

A constitution to determine the practical ground rules of administration. For example, the cooperative ministry might elect
to determine the basic policies from year to year by a vote of the
entire membership, while day-to-day administrative decisions
could be made by an executive committee of ministers and lay
persons from the various ministries.

Certain requirements for new members which would also be
encouraged within the present membership. For example, a commitment to a course of lay education prior to joining the cooperative ministry, an annual decision as to which specialized ministry,
if any, one would participate in, and perhaps a financial commitment.

A provision for the joint administration of present church
facilities.

A stipulation that sufficiently diverse forms of worship be maintained in the Central House to meet the legitimate desires of the
total membership. For example, various forms of the sacrament
could still be administered. Bishops could still receive Episcopal
communicants into the Church.

I am assuming here that the cooperative ministry at the
local level will develop before the denominations reach a
basic consensus on reunification. I would hope that the local
cooperative ministries would feel they could ratify the ultimate decision of the denominations, if such a decision is
ever made. And I would hope, as well, that the individual
denominations would encourage the growth of the cooperative ministry idea.

There is ample biblical precedent for arguing that a properly equipped cooperative ministry is sufficient unto itself in

the sense that it need not be related organically to any wider form of government. The churches originally established by Paul were autonomous, local, cooperative ministries, fully equipped for the administration of the sacraments and the preaching of the Word. But, if we are serious about renewal, we shall have to take two factors into consideration: first, the shape of society requires broader structures to perform ministries that cannot be accomplished on the local level; secondly, the present denominational structure can be transformed to serve an ecumenical Church instead of hindering its development.

Here again we confront the questions of scale and polity. In terms of scale, we have suggested that the cooperative ministry should serve a manageable local area. For purposes of discussion we can define such an area as one that is presently served by anywhere between five and fifteen local congregations. Let us assume that a hypothetical metropolitan area were to inaugurate the cooperative ministry pattern. The present local congregations might be restructured to form a total of ten cooperative ministries, each serving an area equal to one-tenth of the metropolis. The broader unit of the Church would be a Council or Presbytery which would be responsible only for those metropolitan ministries that could not be administered locally. The Council or Presbytery would be made up of representatives of the cooperative ministries. It would thus serve as a center of communication between the various local areas. The local units would determine the need for specialized ministries serving the total area and would contribute to the Presbytery the funds needed to support such ministries.

In turn the Presbyteries (assuming that the pattern developed generally throughout the country) could contribute funds to a national body that would perform *only* those

ministries that could not be achieved at the local or metropolitan level.

If this suggests the scale of the Church, what of the
polity? Generally speaking, the primary locus of power
within the proposed structure would rest with the local cooperative ministry, which would combine elements of the
Free Church and Reformed forms of government. But there
should be certain checks on local autonomy for the sake of
the unity and mission of the whole Church. The following
provisions suggest a viable system of checks and balances:

Ordained ministers would be called by the local ministries,
but their placement would be subject to approval by the Council or
Presbytery.

The Presbytery would serve as a clearing house to enable cooperative ministries in affluent areas to support cooperative ministries in less affluent areas.

Certain local disputes (freedom of the pulpit, controversies for
which no solution is provided in local constitutions, etc.) could
be adjudicated by the Presbyteries.

Positions on issues affecting the gathered ministries (on social
issues affecting the whole metropolis, for example) could be
taken by the Council or Presbytery.

It is not my intention here to create a hard and fast proposal for the polity of a renewed Church. What has been
offered are merely recommendations.

Finally, I would urge consideration of the fruitful role that
bishops might play within a restructured Church. The ap-
pointment of bishops is one means by which the Church
recognizes the mystery of the Incarnation. This sense of
God-become-man is realized primarily in the sacraments of
the Church. The sacraments are the physical manifestation
of spiritual Truth. In the same way, bishops are a physical

manifestation of the spiritual power of Christ in the world. Like bread and wine, bishops possess no uncommon quality within themselves which makes them "out of the ordinary." Nor are bishops necessary to give validity to the sacraments. Even within Roman Catholicism, which recognizes bishops to a far greater extent than does Protestantism, some sacraments may be administered, in extreme cases, by the laity.

I do not suggest that, within Protestantism, the bishop should have temporal authority. But I do maintain that bishops may embody a spiritual authority by virtue of the election of the whole Church and by its investment of such authority in his person. In terms of the proposed structure, bishops would be elected from the ordained clergy by the Presbytery. They would serve as the spokesmen (along with elected lay leaders) for the Church, as pastors to the clergy, and as the receivers of new members into the Body of Christ. They could perform symbolic acts designed to bring the Church into fuller obedience and compassion. Bishops, for example, could establish residence in the depressed areas of the metropolis, exposing themselves to the hardships of the outcast and the wretchedness of communal injustice. Would it compromise a bishop's reputation to make visits to prison, to offer reconciliation amid strife, or to become the third person in a petty institutional quarrel? One thinks of Pope John XXIII. Reluctance about bishops in certain Protestant traditions could turn to deep appreciation if one were to see the need, particularly within today's fragmented Church, for the conferral of spiritual authority on one who is rich in spirit. Unfortunately it is on such matters that we often divide with the most bitter acrimony. If we were to see the Church as mission and allow sensible compromise on less important matters, the difficulty would not seem so great.

10

We began this chapter by asking how the process of renewal might begin with today's local congregations. We have covered a great deal of ground since then. Instead of offering comfort to present institutions, we have offered challenge. But the challenge needs to be made more concrete. If there is any merit in the proposed structure, how do we get there in practice? What might it look like? How would it differ from today's Protestantism?

Let us first ask how we might prove to the skeptics that the underlying idea of the cooperative ministry is feasible. There is only one way, the way of experiment. Actually, what has been suggested is an extension of a concept that has already taken root within a number of areas. The notion of local ecumenism is by no means new or revolutionary, and the complexity of life in the metropolis has already shown many congregations the necessity of joint cooperation. In Chicago, for example, there is the new North Side Cooperative Ministry. To the extent that it has failed, it is because it has not gone far enough. The building that ought to serve as the Central House now serves a large and somewhat ingrown congregation of persons who come from all over the city. The congregation that should serve the artists in the area had not sufficiently considered its task. But there have been successes. A task force from the cooperative ministry has played a vital role in influencing public-school policy. An experimental coffee house, staffed by the laity, has been creating a new image of Christian concern for the uprooted young persons who have moved to the neighborhood. There has been an attempt to pool pastoral resources and to bring lay persons with varying talents together to perform ministries of calling and services for the aged. But it is only a beginning.

What is needed are several demonstration projects. One would be in a smaller town or city. Another would be in a metropolitan suburban area. A third would be in an inner-city neighborhood, and the final experiment would be in a middle-class but fairly sophisticated city neighborhood such as that served by the North Side Cooperative Ministry. If these pilot projects could be started, if we could learn to understand both the challenge and triumph of relevant change, then we could argue the case from experience. It is well to offset any potential skepticism with a remark of Henri Bergson:

> It is useless to maintain that social progress takes place of itself, bit by bit, in virtue of the spiritual condition of the society at a certain point in its history. It is really a leap forward which is only taken when society has made up its mind to try an experiment; this means that society must have allowed itself to be convinced, or at any rate allowed itself to be shaken; and the shake is always given by somebody.

There are plenty of prophets within Protestantism who can give the shake. And one senses that there are an increasing number within the churches who are willing to be shaken.

Pending widespread experimentation, what of the present-day congregation in an area where no other congregations seem interested in cooperation? How is it to function in its isolation? The obvious answer is to initiate conversations with the neighboring congregations; but what if tentative efforts at reaching consensus fail? If this were the best of all possible worlds, such a congregation would be able to engage the services of a national renewal consulting agency which could come, survey needs, suggest a strategy of local mission, and draw up a plan that might serve as a basis for future conversations. I am suggesting here a working group of ecumenical specialists that might even serve as a negotiating team in the first stages of local cooperation. Such a group might be supported by the denominations or establish itself as an independent, not-for-profit corporation. Such an agency would be helpful in encouraging congregational self-study and assisting the Church toward a broader vision of its mission.

Without such resources, a renewal-minded congregation should adopt a posture of waiting combined with a policy of specific symbolic actions. For example, the congregation could inaugurate a specific mission thrust designed to demonstrate its own inability to function without cooperation from the other local churches. It could send representatives (preferably laymen) to denominational meetings to raise questions of ecumenical policy. It could choose a particular ministry of abandonment to show forth a new vision of Christian mission. What it should *not* try to do is too many things at once. The entire strategy should be one of doing one or two things well and at the same time demonstrating the inability of the presently structured local Church to perform all the ministries that need performing.

If we have proposed the skeleton of the renewed Church, we have yet to elaborate its style and content. By understanding more fully what is meant by chaplaincy and teaching, and the implications of abandonment, we shall be able to assess more fully whether the proposed structure is both feasible and worth fighting for.

The local Church today is at a dead end, not because it is totally irrelevant, but because it is cynical to assume that a few bright spots will compensate for the structural weakness of the whole.

Chapter 6
The Church as Chaplain
and Teacher

1

It is popular today to write articles about America's moral decline—the apathy that allows a Catherine Genovese to be murdered before thirty-eight silent witnesses, teenage explosions in city and suburbs, burgeoning premarital sex, price-fixing in the corporations, corruption in the unions, scandal in government, planned obsolescence, initiative-sapping welfare programs—the catalog of sins is infinite. Almost invariably, such analyses of decline suggest that the Church was once among the institutions that guided man through life's intricacies. In the mythology of American culture the task of moral guidance has been conferred on the Church, the home, and the school. The obvious explanation for moral decline today is that the Church, the home, and the school are no longer "doing their job." It may be too simple a diagnosis, but it reflects a popular wisdom too often ignored by the specialists who seek to minister to contemporary ills.

97

The schools are increasingly trapped in a structural milieu, aided and abetted by administrative myopia, that leads to what Paul Goodman has called "compulsory mis-education." Imaginative teachers are often the first to sense the limitations of a system which overcrowds classrooms, burdens front-line educators with back-room bureaucratic form filling, and refuses to demand enough money to do the job that needs doing.

In many cases the home has held up well. It is the most decentralized institution in society. Even within a standardized environment it can set its own standards. If anything, the breakdown of the family may be the result of its having to do too much rather than too little. It must often serve as community, disciplinarian, creative environment, bastion of privacy, center of intimacy, economic provider, and cultural guide in order to fill the void created by a lack of community, culture, and decent relationships in the wider world. Whatever the causes, the divorce statistics, if they can be believed, provide an alarming index of the family's inability to remain stable, and of the parents' difficulty in exercising positive influence on their children.

One senses that if a breakdown in Church, home, and school continues, the total society will either be the locus of revolutionary upheaval, or the state will gradually assume more and more authority. The problems to date have seemed greater than the proposed solutions. Nevertheless, revolution is a last resort, and the prospect of vastly increased state domination is not a happy one. The effort to renew existing structures and to create new ones where present forms are obsolete becomes the only responsible strategy.

In a pluralistic society Protestantism can be expected to fill only a partial role in a total strategy of renewal. Nevertheless, practically any dormant institution today that undergoes the test of renewal will set a pattern for other institutions. Even a specialized society is profoundly influenced as its specific sectors undergo change.

2

In this chapter we are considering the Church as a resource. Chaplaincy and teaching are resource ministries. Taken together they comprise an indispensable aspect of the Church on mission. They are the mind and soul of the Church, even as abandonment represents the physical action of the Church in the world. They are resources that ought to be made available to every Church member, and it is as criminal to deny them within the precincts of the Church as it is to deny basic education in the schools and basic food to the starving.

There is truth in the allegation that the Church, like the home and the school, has exercised scant influence in creating the basic values that could sustain a just and human society. Today's Church is looked to less and less as a resource in facing the moral dilemmas of individual and corporate existence. The harassed parent, the businessman with vocational conflicts, the couple edging toward divorce —all tend to look elsewhere for guidance, or else to look nowhere. One could explain that Protestants are just as confused as the rest of the world. But this would be begging the question of whether a more effective job can be done.

Consider first the persons on whom the job of chaplaincy and teaching now falls. For the most part they are the professionally trained ministers. Are they equipped to preach, to teach, to counsel? Consider the typical portfolio of the contemporary pastor. He is expected to do at least five things.

He should be a dynamic and inspiring preacher who spends at least a day or two each week studying and preparing his sermon. He ought to be an accomplished speaker, a good writer, and acquainted enough with the world to integrate biblical insight and contemporary understandings in his preaching.

He should be an accomplished administrator, aggressive yet diplomatic, alert to every phase of the Church's programming. He should be able to delegate authority. He ought to have a sophisticated grasp of structure and a quick capacity for logistics.

He should be a competent counselor. He should have enough training to discriminate between those he can help and those who ought to be referred to more specialized professionals. He should keep up with literature in the field. He should have highly developed sensitivity to individual problems. And he ought to be available to counsel his parishioners at any hour of the day.

He needs also to be a pastor, one who keeps in touch with his far-flung flock, who broods over their individual needs, who visits them when sick, who baptizes children, performs marriages, and conducts funerals. And, for good measure, he should call frequently on the total membership.

Then he must be a teacher. Presumably his preaching and counseling prepare him to administer programs of adult education, to handle confirmation classes and to maintain a relationship with the Sunday School. But ought he not also to have certain specialized areas of ability? Perhaps to lead discussions among the men of the Church on the relation of Christian faith to work, or among the women on the feminine mystique?

These are the basic expectations of the competent pastor. But this is by no means the whole job description. He must also be, depending on circumstance, a chauffeur, a willing attender of every organization's weekly or monthly meeting, a skilled diplomat, and a liturgist. If he has any standing at all, he must participate in the wider activities of the Church. This means serving on a board of directors or attending denominational meetings. If the minister has any sense that the Church is not quite what it ought to be, he probably participates in social action projects in the community at large. In order to satisfy his need for privacy (or to live up to the congregation's image of him as a moral paragon) our clergyman must also be a good husband and father, devoting adequate time to his family.

Would it be overly critical to suggest that such a job description is absurd? In the first place it is never realized. In the second place it imposes impossible expectations on the cleric and adds to his burden of pathological guilt when he fails to function well.

Since this job description applies to practically the entire professional arm of the Church (save for the few who are trained and employed to work in specialized ministries) the notion of the Church as a resource suffers a severe blow. Several solutions have been advanced to change this pattern without fundamentally changing Church structure. Some have advanced the idea that the minister should be seen as a "pastoral director"—a resource person to laymen in the Church who would be called on to carry out many of the functions that now burden the minister. The pastoral director would make laymen responsible for such jobs as calling, assisting in worship, and education. He would insist that organizations in the Church be run by lay persons rather than by himself. He would refuse to carry on administrative functions that could be assumed by the laity.

The notion of the pastoral director is not bad in itself. It is a militant rejection of the minister as an ecclesiastical errand boy. To some extent it frees him to preach and to teach. In fact a number of clergymen have succeeded in implementing this sort of redefinition of responsibility in the local setting.

But consider the odds against such an approach as a basic strategy of renewal.

The first fact that must be stated bluntly is that the proportion of clergymen able to perform effectively as pastors (or as pastoral directors) is at most one-half of those currently serving local churches. It is really amazing that there are as many good ministers as there are. But the fact remains that there are many who are simply unequipped—whether emotionally or educationally—with the talents needed for the ministry of chaplaincy and teaching. This is a rash judgment and of necessity it must be a subjective one. One suspects most ministers concur. They are no more fond of the current job description than they are able to fill it.

Yes, the notion of the pastoral director may hold back the dike for a time. The glowing description of the minister as one who has a foot in the Church, a foot in the world, may provide a nice ego ideal. But sooner or later the structure is seen to militate against the best efforts of those who minister. The local congregation is generally too small to afford the services of men and women who could perform all of the necessary tasks. Given the lack of cooperative ministries through which the talents of many are shared by many, seminaries can scarcely train persons for the specialized tasks that must be fulfilled. So, in a real sense, the Gospel is smothered by the present structure, and St. Paul's differentiation of ministries is ignored.

It is true that style is as important as structure. One wishes that all ministers would adopt a more contemporary stance, would doff their embarrassed reserve for long enough to converse in down-to-earth terms with man, would see the Church as mission, would cease the cliquish practice of nursing their gripes with their colleagues and never sharing their hopes and doubts in public. One hopes and sees a gradual change in style emerging. There is a sharper new breed of clergyman, alert to the world about him, discriminating in what he emphasizes, able to gain the respect of his congregation, socially militant yet sensitive to less dramatic needs. Structure is not king, and it is finally people who sound the deepest transformations. Can we not hope in this? Perhaps we can. Those on the inside can bask, in the sense that things are changing bit by bit. Today's competent minister may himself vigorously defend the status quo because, after all, things are going well from his point of view. Why rock the boat? And the whole debate could end with a glorious reassertion of the old Protestant practice of muddling through so as not to offend anyone. There could be a big meeting to reassert The Way We Do Things. An *avant garde* drama group could be brought in from the fringes to prove that We Really Don't Neglect Culture.

But we cannot avoid the structural problem so easily.

3

Today's minister is plainly not equipped to perform the tasks of chaplaincy and teaching. His seminary has trained him in a little bit of everything. Even if he has had the foresight to specialize, most local churches will force upon him the outmoded job definition we have described. Given the cooperative ministry structure, however, the whole training process could be revised. The first year of seminary could be a basic introduction which would be as relevant to lay persons as to potential ministers. One would enter seminary not knowing necessarily what one would eventually do: perhaps a tent-making ministry of the type Gordon Cosby describes, a ministry of abandonment, or possibly the ministry of chaplaincy or teaching. After one year the layman would be able to leave a wiser man. The second year would be more specialized. A decision would be forthcoming. What is to be one's special area of ministry? The third year would be in the field, in a cooperative ministry such as we have described. The candidate for chaplaincy would be immersed in the worship and preaching ministry of the Church. The candidate for a specialized ministry of teaching or pastoral care would be immersed in that. One who aspired to the ministry of abandonment would gain important experience.

After a year in the field, a final decision would be made. Is the student to continue? If not, he is prepared to be a responsible layman. If so, he makes a solid choice of a field. His final year gives him the specific academic preparation needed to perform his chosen task. This could be flexible. The seminaries would learn exactly how long it takes to train for one or another specialty. Programs would be tailored accordingly.

Many seminaries would object, arguing that the seminary is both a training center *and* a serious academic institution where advanced scholarly work is pursued. Teachers whose primary interest is in research might rebel at so close a potential relationship to the needs of the Church-at-large. But the seminaries must consider the possibility that specialized centers, preferably related to the great universities, should be developed to carry on the vitally important task of theological, biblical, and historical scholarship. There need not be a total divorce of the practical and the academic. Indeed, many highly competent teachers might welcome a chance to move from one environment to the other, and, through visiting lecturers, the restructured seminaries could maintain contact with the most advanced scholarly thought. Indeed, in the most academically inclined seminaries today, students for the ministry tend to be shortchanged, due to the preoccupation of the more eminent professors with graduate work. This results, in some cases, in a tutor system through which much of the grading and classroom work is handled by graduate students.

4

But how can the seminaries move if Church structure remains stagnant? One way to move the churches, and thus the seminaries, is to project what things would be like under the new system. What, for example, would the new teaching ministry of the Church look like?

On a purely visual level the teaching ministry might have several appearances. Decentralization and specialization would allow for the adaptation of traditional church buildings for use as *permanent teaching centers*. Classrooms could be created to suggest the subject matter, and imaginative use could be made of other spaces. The sanctuary, for example, could be used for audio-visuals, the halls as galleries, one room as a library, another as a studio. This would be a welcome change for those churches that try to make one room double for eight different purposes, or throw the entire Sunday School into an acoustically horrendous enclosure for an hour a week, hoping that curtains and other devices will enable seven separate classes to function harmoniously. The adaptation of present church buildings for full-time teaching purposes is only one alternative. Apartments, storefronts, and houses could also serve as teaching facilities.

A more important consideration is who would be doing the teaching. No longer would the few competent professionals and volunteer teachers in a neighborhood be scattered about in separate churches trying to shore up separate educational programs. They would be attached to the neighborhood teaching centers. Specially trained professionals would devote full time to the teaching mission. In such a setting, only the truly interested volunteers would be trained to handle various phases of the program. In short, the educational ministry would be in the hands of ministers and laymen whose talent and interest lie in teaching.

This structure would replace the Sunday School and the slipshod adult programs in local churches. Classes could be held when convenient for community residents. Curriculum could be broadened to fit specific interests. Much of the course material could be developed locally, thus increasing its relevance. One of the sad facts today is that even the best denominational materials are most often useless at the local level because teachers lack the basic training and outlook to respond fully to the materials that are provided. Also, the nationally developed curriculums are often utterly irrelevant to specific local situations. Through the development of local competence, a genuine diversity could be attained in course offerings for youth, children, and adults. Given adequate budgets, the teaching centers could afford high-quality audio-visual material—the better contemporary films, etc. In educationally depressed areas, the centers could serve children in need of tutoring. The possibilities are endless, and the heart of the proposal is its assumption that a cooperative ministry will be sufficiently self-determining to tailor its combined talents to the specific needs of the community.

The teaching ministry would not be aimed solely at producing an educated Protestant laity. In many cases its mission would fall under the heading of abandonment. The teaching centers could be flexible enough to open their doors to the entire community. Social action groups in the community could conduct classes. A group of mothers could experiment with a Montessori school. Public-school teachers, university professors, and others could offer courses that they have wanted for years to experiment with. In this way the teaching Church would be a center of dialogue with the world rather than a closed institution operated for the sole benefit of members.

One final point: To teach well is to be faithful to one's subject. It is also to be open to debate. The worst stereotype that hovers over the present teaching of Protestantism is that it is propagandistic and conversion-oriented, less interested in adding to one's knowledge than in filling the mind with unexamined beliefs and memorized maxims. This is to defeat the purpose of education, which is to stir the student's curiosity and help him to exercise his own talents. If the teaching of the Church is faithful to subject matter it will leave the student the freedom to accept or reject. Part of the reason why present Protestant teaching is so stultified is that it assumes it must also preach and moralize. By structuring the Church in the way we have suggested, teaching is freed to become teaching. By recognizing teaching as one of the three root ministries of the Church, there would be a boost in morale for the religious educators who, for so long, have been confined to the ghetto of the archaic Sunday School.

On the metropolitan level, teaching would express itself in the establishment of training centers for laymen who seek to minister in the specialized areas of the emerging city. Ecumenical retreat centers would also play an important role within the new structure. Doctors and lawyers and, indeed, all vocational groups could be brought together to explore their separate and joint ministry to the world. And, contrary to today's forms, the new structure—through the ministries of abandonment—would give laymen the organizational basis by which to move from reflection to action.

Compare today's structure with the one proposed. Even if lay people in a given metropolis are brought into study

programs (whether denominational or ecumenical), they
are hard-pressed to move from reflection to action. Why?
Primarily because action requires organization and organization requires money. Suppose, for example, that a group
of thirty lay persons in a given city meets for six months and
determines that their mission for the next year is to fight
air pollution, primarily because no one else is fighting it and
because, unchecked, it can do as much ultimate damage to
people as any other evil. They need fifteen thousand dollars
to get started. They have three choices. They can go to
their respective denominations for approval of the project,
but the chances are that approval would take at least a
year and that within this time the group's impetus would
diminish. They can decide to do the job on their own, possibly withdrawing their support from the Church in order to
raise the necessary funds. In this case they are denied the
resources of the Church; they find the Church an impedi-
ment. Or, under the proposed structure—the cooperative
ministry—they could constitute themselves as a task force
and go to the cooperative ministry for the approval, on an
annual basis, of such *ad hoc* programs as battling air pollution, fighting for decent housing, etc. The cooperative ministry would be prepared to operate with more speed than the
divided denominations. Since the laity would initiate the
project and staff it with volunteer help, there would not be
the present pattern of setting up professionalized denominational offices to deal with such issues. Indeed, one of the
problems with "official" denominational offices is that they
do not represent a grass roots constituency, and the persons
they seek to influence know it. Built into the structure of the
cooperative ministries—and the metropolitan structures that
would support the local ministries—would be the assumption that study leads to action. Therefore, there might be
ten task forces in a metropolitan area. All of them could

appeal for support from the whole Church. And support would be contingent on the approval of the whole Church, either in the local community or in the metropolis at large.

Teaching thus becomes the bridge between chaplaincy and abandonment. The teaching or training structures would be seen as part of the process by which the Christian moves from celebration and seeking to involvement and action. And the traffic would be two way.

5

The second resource the restructured church could offer is that of chaplaincy. We refer to the preaching, music, liturgy, and the pastoral counseling of the Church. As in teaching, our proposed structure would free those with talent in these areas to perform effectively and without the burden of too many other responsibilities. We can begin by raising two questions about the effect of the proposed structure on the mission of chaplaincy. We have concentrated the chaplaincy function in a "Central House" and suggested that two ministers be entrusted with primary responsibility as preachers and worship leaders in the community. The first question is whether the present local church structure does not have the advantage of offering more variety. The second question is what effect the new structure would have on the pastoral relationship of minister to people that now exists to some extent within local churches.

If anything, the proposed structure would increase the depth and variety of the Church's worship life. The Central House would be a worship center, but it would offer numerous varieties of worship, and its preaching would not be confined to the two clergymen. Ministers and laymen attached to the teaching and abandonment missions would provide a pool of talent that could be drawn upon. There would also be access to guest preachers and worship leaders. One could envision a variety of services during the week and at various times of the day. Some might be built around music, others around prayer, and others around the sacraments. Liturgical experiments could be attempted, and there could be a rebirth of congregational participation. But let us not play down the persons who would be in charge of the preaching and worship life of the Central House. They would be selected precisely because of their talent. Freed from other responsibilities, they might not become George Buttricks, William Sloane Coffins, or Kelly Miller Smiths overnight, but they would be several notches above the present average.

The benefit of having a few preachers of genuine ability available on a full-time basis to a total community offsets the advantages of being able to pick and choose among ten or fifteen clergymen who hardly have time to write a sermon. A more serious observation in favor of the proposal exists: The preacher within the new structure would be under an obligation that scarcely exists in the contemporary Church. He would be a preacher to the community. He would be obliged to take such a role with utmost seriousness. Freed to perform his vocation, liberated from the necessity of institutional promotion, he would bear the high responsibility of opening the Word to a whole people. In his priestly role it is he who would preach the reconciling Word. As one obliged to consider the full implication of Scripture, it is he who would be called to fill the need of a seeking people. As one alert to the challenges to faith that haunt each personality, including his own, he would be entrusted with the pastoral task of presenting the brokenness of man before the gracious altar of God. One such full-time preaching pastor would be worth one thousand part-time ones. It would be parochial indeed to speak of a "preacher to the whole community" without recognizing that the Central House would be an appropriate place to continue the dialogue that has begun to develop among Protestants, Catholics, and Jews. Let the Central House become a beacon of a true ecumenism on the part of Protestantism; let it be the visible symbol of Protestantism's will toward true brotherhood! The possibilities are endless.

But would not such a system be impersonal? It might, but it need not be. The outreach missions of the cooperative ministry would be able to carry on a certain amount of worship life if it seemed desirable. Pastoral relations would exist within the centers of teaching and abandonment. But let us examine the matter from a different perspective. If one sees counseling as a basic ingredient in a pastoral relationship, the present system is scarcely adequate. One may know one's minister in today's church, but how many would entrust him with a deep personal problem? If one is truly in need of personal guidance one looks for two things: professional competence and the security of relative anonymity. Neither of these is assured within the local church setting. A measure of counseling does go on, and it is often useful, but very rarely do those most in need dare to venture into the minister's study. Under the new system, professional competence would be a mark of counseling services. Anonymity would be facilitated. And one would be assured of the availability of competent counseling.

6

Another question presents itself. Would not the emphasis on chaplaincy and teaching suggested here create a specialized clergy even more divorced from the concerns of laymen than today's ministers? It would create a competent clergy, but hardly an isolated one. In fact, it takes little imagination to speculate on the common mission that would develop among clergy and laymen working together in specific areas. The very structure of the cooperative ministry would open up many positions to laymen that have traditionally been the preserve of the ordained clergy. Laymen who happen also to be teachers might find the no-holds-barred educational ministry to be the very vocational option they have been looking for. Psychiatrists who have cried out for a decentralization of bureaucratized and often inaccessible mental health facilities might welcome employment in the local pastoral centers. Practically any profession or trade could prove an integral resource to the ministries of abandonment. Indeed it is the laymen who would grow in responsibility. There is no reason why one who does not preach and administer sacraments should be ordained. The number of ordained ministers within a cooperative structure could, in fact, be less than half the professional staff. One should add that—with a new birth of vitality and specialization in the seminaries—there is no reason why more than half the graduates of theological institutions should be ordained. The real source of clericalism within Protestantism is the isolation of the minister within the present local Church structure. He is so alone and so often misunderstood that he tends to have no social existence, no warm friendship, except with other clergymen. A hostility between clergy and laity develops. Often it is unconscious and subtle. But it has about the same bad consequences as the cliquishness of American foreign service officers overseas who isolate themselves from the language and interests of those whom they seek to serve.

7

In this chapter and the last we have spoken of the Church as a local cooperative ministry serving a definable neighborhood, whether in city, suburban, or rural areas. Naturally such ministries would develop differently in different locales. In affluent suburbs there might be a greater need for teaching and chaplaincy than for local ministries of abandonment, since many suburbanites could more profitably serve in inner-city areas or in specialized ministries affecting the total metropolis. In rural areas the concentration of churches might not be large enough to support a cooperative ministry in a given town, although rural ecumenicity of any sort would be preferable to the present prospect of dying denominational churches trying to support themselves through their death agony. The rural mission of the Church could concentrate on preparing persons for the inevitable move to the city.

What must be kept steadfastly in mind is that the principle of decentralization places basic emphasis on local initiative. Our hypothetical example and our suggestions have been evocative rather than rigid. We assume that new life will emerge, and appropriate new forms will develop if persons at the grass roots are given a flexible structure and the power to see things through at the local level. The most debilitating result of contemporary organization throughout society is the loss of individual control over destiny. Only when people are given responsibility for their own affairs and the means of implementing their creative ideas is there much hope of reviving this sense of initiative.

It is an interesting exercise to briefly examine the effect of our proposed structure on the deficiencies outlined in the first chapters of this book. We shall list the deficiencies and suggest concisely the antidotes implicit in the cooperative ministry structure. Here we shall consider those objections that could be remedied by the implementation of the Church's mission as chaplain and teacher, reserving the implications of abandonment for the next chapter.

1) *The denominational Church is competitive and repetitive.* The cooperative structure eliminates competition and varies program and mission from place to place.

2) *There is too little lay participation in substantive decision-making.* The cooperative ministry localizes policy and program decisions, increasing lay participation.

3) *Seminaries are divorced from the Church.* The cooperative ministry makes provision for the integral participation of seminary students and professors, and for lay education in seminaries.

4) *Church membership is time-consuming and concerned with the trivial.* The cooperative ministry scales down institutional maintenance and bases participation on interest and talent.

5) *The Church is a private preserve of the membership.* The cooperative ministry opens its buildings to the public, identifies them by function, and has the resources to make its programs known to the entire community.

6) *The Church's worship is without rhyme or reason.* The quality of worship is enhanced by the "Central House" concept, and there is a wider range of specialized worship services. Preaching and music are improved, and one can attend without feeling the obligation to contribute or join.

7) *The Church is not concerned with deep issues.* The teaching ministry is structured to allow the community to raise the issues it is concerned about and is equipped to

offer both competent teaching and open-ended debate.

8) *The Church is not a community*. The various arms of the cooperative ministry provide the structural basis for five essential types of community: local loyalty, consensus, reconciliation, spontaneous association, and intimate living together. Residential communities, for example, could easily spring up around specialized ministries.

One can also reflect on the impact of new structures on several of the most cherished functions that have been traditionally assigned to the Church:

1) *Proclaiming the Gospel*. C. Kilmer Myers has noted that the only facility needed for this is a tent and an altar. John Wesley did without both. We provide a more weatherproof roof, the possibility of a more educated laity to hear the Word, and a ministry whose sole vocation is to preach it.

2) *Showing forth unity in Christ*. Practically any polity would accomplish this more visibly than does denominationalism. Ours builds on St. Paul's assumption that diverse functions must be performed in order to maintain a healthy body.

3) *Evangelism*. This task can be performed only by redefining what it means to evangelize. One implication of our approach is that the Church is not called to place great emphasis on "winning souls." If the mere verbal confession of Christ as Lord and Savior is the goal of evangelism, Christianity becomes a hollow superstition and the Church becomes an earthly accountant for a God who has ceased to exist in any meaningful sense. Our proposed structure invests the chaplaincy with the formal proclamation of the Word. But it assumes that teaching and abandonment are equally important to the creation of that transformed vision which marks Christian consciousness. A renewed Church will probably be wise to forget the term evangelism for a

few decades until the structures of the Church show forth
the fruits of faith a bit more plainly. Then there will be
something to evangelize about.

8

One can conclude by pointing to the obvious. There is
nothing sacred in the present structure of Protestantism.
Even when set against traditional understandings of mission, it falters. When one considers, in addition, the necessity
of making the Church relevant to today's world, traditional
forms are seen as a total anachronism.

Responsible decentralization requires that we enumerate
tasks that cannot be performed on the local level. What sorts
of centralization would be needed to further increase the
church's effectiveness as chaplain and teacher? How might
such centralization occur without creating the bureaucratic
overlay and multiple staffing that make present-day denominationalism so cumbersome? It would be impossible
within these pages to discuss every contingency, so we shall
try to define some basic principles and illustrate them with
specific examples.

The first principle—remember we are speaking here of
chaplaincy and teaching—is that no function ought to be
assumed by a more central administration if it can be
handled and administered locally. Thus, for example, specialized ministries, such as hospital chaplaincies or college
work, should ideally be a part of the cooperative ministry
in the given locale of the hospital or university, even if
salaries are paid for with outside funds.

There are, however, aspects of chaplaincy and teaching
that require more centralized structures serving a wider
area. There might, for example, be a city-wide service for

anyone tempted to commit suicide, a retreat center that could be shared by a number of cooperative ministries, a publication that linked the various ministries together by outlining the needs of the total area. Such central functions would be tailored to the expressed needs of combined cooperative ministries in order to avoid the debilitating situation of having ideas and policies imposed upon the churches from above. In some cases such imposition may be necessary if a given group of churches is deliberately flaunting minimal Christian standards. This is one reason for the suggestion of a Presbytery structure, as outlined in the preceding chapter. But it is generally better to build these standards into local constitutions and polities rather than to legislate them from offices far removed from the scene of trouble.

Once the local structures are in place, the possibilities of inventive approaches to the total geographic area are infinite. Certainly one area in which the localized teaching ministry would falter, for example, is in serving the needs of workers in business and industry and the professions who need highly specialized approaches to the problems of humanizing the work environment. Also, in big cities, there is probably a need for centralized volunteer training programs that can send laymen into special areas of need, equipped to do more than wield a paint brush and weep over the plight of the poor. Ministries in radio and television —if they can be made truly imaginative—might also be beyond the bounds of cooperative ministries.

At the national level there would still be need for retreat centers and other national gathering places so that persons from the whole country could gather to study and reflect on national issues. It might be possible to begin a series of evangelical academies such as exist in Germany. Some sort of agency would be needed to fill in the gaps where local cooperation does not exist or where the challenges are too great to be met by local and regional ministries. A national forum which would present Church positions on national policy would be useful if it represented the position of a majority of local ministries. Cooperative ministries could send representatives to an annual national meeting in order to determine *ad hoc* emphases from year to year.

Certain costly and relatively ineffective programs presently conducted by national denominations could be eliminated. National departments of religious education would have questionable value, since planning and curriculum development would be local and regional. Pension departments could be consolidated. Stewardship (fund raising) departments would be inessential. Even under present conditions, their cost outweighs their effectiveness. Most publishing efforts would be eliminated in favor of less expensive locally published magazines dealing with substantive issues rather than institutional promotion. National radio and television departments would be scaled down, particularly those not presently sponsored ecumenically. They draw funds from local efforts and have produced little of permanent value anyway. Funds from presently owned church trusts, stock holdings, endowments, etc. could be used to encourage the development of effective decentralized units. A coordinated ecumenical fund could replace competitive church extension departments and offer low-interest building loans to cooperative ministries in areas where it could be proved beyond doubt that the building would be used for mission. Again the principle of decentralization is the basic rule of thumb. What remains of present structures will remain by virtue of its ability to contribute to the mission of a Church which is united at its base.

Perhaps this seemingly abrupt rejection of much that happens on today's national level will seem more charitable if one adds that those who presently do a good deal of competitive shoring up of departments nationally might function better and be more fulfilled personally if they were given substantive local responsibility.

Insofar as the Church is a resource to the laity and to the community, it will emphasize chaplaincy and teaching. This is, for the most part, though not exclusively, a ministry to those human needs that remain constant. But the Church must also be in the world of change, of revolution, of sudden need, and of daily contingency. Here it must assume its most flexible posture. It is here that we move from chaplaincy and teaching to the theory and strategy of abandonment.

Chapter 7
The Way of
Abandonment

1

I have already sketched in several places the implications of abandonment as the strategy by which the Church relates most fully to the world. The relationship, it should be evident, is always to be understood as a two-way street. The Church does not relate to the world as a condescending Magic Father with special gifts to give. Instead, it draws its cue from Jesus Christ, who admonished those He helped to remain silent about it. Abandonment draws its cue from the sacrificial acts of our Lord, culminating in crucifixion.

The self-giving of God to His creation is at once open and hidden. It is open in the sense that it is free. There are no strings attached. It is open because it expresses itself in the supreme willingness to ask forgiveness for those who crucify. It is open because, in Christ, God allows no one to suggest that His gift is qualified in any way.

But the giving, the abandonment, is hidden as well. It is

hidden because it does not proclaim itself. The gift is its own proclamation. It is hidden because its existence as a gift is known only to those who realize that the only possible response is unqualified thanks. Those who choose not to recognize it are free to go their way. Such self-giving is the very essence of the divine mystery. It leaves man free to accept or reject the incalculable, infinite mercy of God. The gift combines a totally irrational divine poetry with equally irrational self-expression in a wholly human crucifixion. Hidden or open, this gift is the supreme abandonment.

And yet, for the Church to claim sole custodianship of the gift is the supreme negation of its reality. The Church possesses the gift only insofar as its members respond to the open and hidden character of the gift itself. Insofar as the Church proclaims the gift openly, it does so with no strings attached. It points to this all-consuming mercy and to its availability. But, the Church's proclamation must also hide itself in the form of unqualified giving to the world. It is this unheralded giving to the world that marks the true Church. It is the sort of giving that asks nothing in return, that does not seek to explain itself in innumerable institutional press releases, that is self-effacing and, in its own way, mysterious and surprising. So the point of departure in discussing abandonment is Christ Himself and the hidden and open character of His giving. Always the distinction must be made between the chaplaincy and teaching that is appropriate to those whose eyes are being opened, who now ask the ultimate questions, and, on the other hand, the distinctly evangelical task of going forth into the world to create appropriate parables which, themselves, begin to open eyes and provoke questions.

2

But there is a danger that lurks close to the surface of such an approach and which must be immediately exposed and eliminated. It is not the danger of being misunderstood, for misunderstanding is bound to cloud any relevant abandonment of the Church to the world. Neither is it the possibility of suffering. The danger is that anonymous, self-giving abandonment on the part of the Church will reveal itself to be smug, self-righteous, and pompous. Such self-righteousness would result from a failure to accept the gift in all of its radical absoluteness. It would reveal itself as a clinging to vestiges of moralism, institutionalism, and cheap grace in the implicit statement, "See how righteous I am! I give without asking in return. I engage in suffering because I will it. I represent a new, relevant religious emphasis." The nature of the gift, rightly perceived, should banish these superstitious and demonic illusions, but the tendency of the Church is always to debase the gift in order to claim an authoritative *raison d'être* for all of its activities.

There is only one protection against the debilitating process which abandonment can undergo in the hands of sinful men and women, and that is the recovery of the essentially searching and exploratory nature of Christian life itself. This involves the recognition, outlined in Chapter Four, that it is impossible for the Church to proclaim that God's victory is divorced from the continual working out of His will within the fabric of history. This means that the Church, while it can rejoice in what has already been done, while it can point to biblical revelation and be glad in it, must always seek God in the now, and see the fundamentally future nature of salvation. Indeed, the Church, to be obedient, must always define salvation in terms of faith, in terms of what one can hope for on the basis of what has happened and what is happening. Once this is understood; once the moving, active character of the biblical God has been freed from the clutches of a Church that continually wishes to define salvation in the past tense, there can be no alternative but to seek a correlation between what the Church already knows and what God is now saying within the fabric of life and history. The Christian life becomes the search for the delineations of God's grace, for the perimeters of His purpose in the world. Only when the evangelistic nature of abandonment is seen as identical to its searching nature will the pitfalls of pride and works-righteousness be minimized.

Thus the Church relates to the world because it is interested in what God is doing and saying. We must reject the strain of Christian thought that says the Church and the world have nothing in common. We must challenge, on the theological rather than on the merely ethical level, those who would maintain that the only task of the Church is to gather into its bosom those souls who are predestined, or willing, to forsake the confused evil world for the unconfused, good atmosphere of the ecclesiastical establishment. The liberal Protestant reaction to pietistic otherworldliness and separatism has often been so extreme and immature that the basic theological issue has been submerged. The optimistic Protestant liberal will argue that the world is God's creation, that it is good, indeed that it is holy! From this enthusiastic vantage point he will solve his theological problem by asserting dogmatically that the Church can have nothing to say to this good creation. Such an argument is raised to a pseudotheological level by those who would make the world into the sole source of revelation and take its sociological and economic patterns as normative expressions of divine will.

The God whom the Church has emasculated is proclaimed as dead, and the world becomes the new God. The Docetism of the Church, its tendency to make Jesus into an other-worldly but perceptibly Anglo-Saxon mirage, is countered by the Arianism of the uncritical secularists who rightly discern the motions of Jesus within the fabric of history and wrongly absolutize these human intuitions into what they regard as the only perceptible reality. Like fringe political groups more interested in making noise than winning, the *avant garde* Protestants laugh in the comfort of their new and relevant idols. This naïve approach allows the so-called "conservative wing" of Protestantism to get away with another sort of worldliness by proclaiming that Christ has nothing to do with the world and that, implicitly, the National Association of Manufacturers, the Daughters of the American Revolution, and the American Medical Association have nothing to fear.

The sad reality is that the conservatives are quite correct in suggesting that the world we live in is damned, fallen, evil, and subject to a tragic flaw. It is a reasonable suggestion in the light of history and of the biblical exposure of the divine dimension of history. It becomes unreasonable only when it limits the power of God to suffer man, in his freedom, to be responsible to this dying world. Reinhold Niebuhr has pointed out persuasively the dangers of both uncritical optimism and uncritical pessimism in relation to human destiny. The one leads to unreflective involvment in secular ideologies, the other to an equally unreflective withdrawal.

Christians are called to be aware of the mixture of good and evil that exists in every man, in every community, in every nation, and in every interaction of every person and group. Nature, too, provides a similar panorama of good and evil—the necessity of death and slaughter in order to preserve the "balance" of nature. In nature and society, demonic forces vie with weakened goodness, and the Christian attributes escape from destruction to grace—not to some simple Lone Ranger Grace which comes riding up to stay the hand on the button but to something that is active in the world, in the face of all of man's blundering, to keep hope alive. If such grace chooses to work through fire and storm, through an agnostic scientist or a Communist ruler, through the freedom movement or the U.S. Senate, that is its prerogative. The delineations of that grace are hardly contiguous with the boundaries of the institutional Church.

It is the Christian's responsibility to affirm this working grace wherever it exists and to fight its opposite to the limits of his flawed ability. The very complexity of the search means that he is partially protected—if he sees his task as search rather than the implementation of something he knows for sure—from the dangers of self-righteousness, particularly in its institutional form. He does not go forth from the sanctuary to prove, but to seek. He does not look for merit badges. He goes because God has gone before him. At least, that is his hope and his faith.

And because God's grace *is* manifest in the world to eyes of faith, the Christian will, in going forth, be constrained to be grateful for what God is saying in the life of the world. He will see the relation as a two-way street. And he will find that it is precisely in this interaction that the Gospel becomes a living reality rather than a moribund subject in a professional curriculum.

3

Biblically speaking, abandonment to the needs and concerns of the world is not primarily a means of helping mankind but provides a perspective from which to judge the smugness and unconcern of the religious establishment. The travail of humanity is God's continuing judgment on the unconcern of the religious. Christ did not reject the religious establishment. He sought to purify it. That is why He threw the money-changers out of the temple. That is why He rejected the Pharisee in favor of the prostitute. And one senses that the only means of purifying the halls of religiosity is to tread the paths of the world, pointing continually to the depths of human anguish and injustice.

Abandonment suggests that the most profound moral teaching of the Church is not primarily words but action. The Church speaks to the world not so much in myriad racial pronouncements, as when ministers are killed in the course of their abandonment to a just cause. Indeed the whole discussion of Christian ethics has been hung up on the question, "What can we say?" when a more appropriate question is, "What shall we do?" or better, "What shall we be?" An interesting, if embarrassing, example of the futility of words alone occurred at a recent national meeting of the United Church of Christ. In an unexpected move, several representatives of the civil rights movement in Chicago arrived at the denominational assembly to lay their grievances before the delegates. As they walked from the front of the room following their presentation, the chairman of the meeting said, "Thank you. We hope to have a statement on public education before the end of the meeting." The sad fact was not that the denomination failed to take a more concrete stand, but that, under the circumstances, it was impotent to take *any* stand other than the promise of a statement—to be filed away in its archives.

Abandonment suggests that the ethical posture of the Church has more to do with parable than with statements of moral principles, absolutes, and norms. The plain fact is that most statements adopted by the religious establishment have virtually no effect on the status quo. Only when they are implemented do they become significant. Ethics by parable —we might call it descriptive ethics—has a biblical origin. Ethical possibility is never seen in the abstract; it is always related to the human realities of the moment. Consider, for example, the Parable of the Good Samaritan. Christ simply described a situation in which two highly placed persons scorned an injured man's cry for help. An unlikely prospect from Samaria came to his aid. The ethical relevance of this and other New Testament parables depends on where we find ourselves in the reality that Christ describes. If we identify with the Samaritan, we are more likely to be the neighbor in a similar situation. Our sympathy is with the underdog. But the Church's typical reaction to this story has been to commend the Samaritan and tell us to be like him. We do not change so simply. Descriptive ethics is the process of locating ourselves within a specific situation. If we are to change at all, if we are to gain our freedom, we must know what the situation is, who the characters are, and where we stand. Parables do not tell one what to do. They are not neat little maxims. They tell what some persons do in some situations. The story of the Good Samaritan treats us to the nice irony that elevates the outsider and the misfit above the respectable citizenry in the upside-down order of Jesus Christ.

The standards we endorse are more often than we like to admit the result of our clinging to a self-image, to a model, or to some person whom we aspire to imitate. All that we do becomes an act of worship, the imitation of a certain style, whether for good or ill. Parables help us to discern the hidden depths within ourselves that correspond to the styles revealed by others. They are the profoundest of communications. The ministry of abandonment is the creation of appropriate parables.

4

Considered in relation to the present structures of the Church, abandonment very definitely implies a radical curtailment of many pursuits that, in Gordon Cosby's terms, "protect the Church from crucifixion." We have posited in our proposed Church structure the literal abandonment of most church construction to free funds for mission in the world. In fact, the term abandonment—applied to current institutional Protestantism—refers mostly to the sorting out of ballast that can be jettisoned to enable the Church to move in a positive direction. This sort of abandonment is painful. It is what the ecumenical discussions among the denominations will come to if they are really serious about unity and renewal. Will the Methodists give up their printing presses if they are no longer needed? Will the Episcopalians give up some of their institutional baggage? Will the Presbyterians? Will the pinciple of abandonment operate when the cumbersome fund-raising apparatus of the various churches is merged, scaled down, decentralized, or eliminated? Are the various denominations prepared to give up some of their plans, their aspirations, their structures, for the sake of a renewed Church? The old terminology provides an out. There is no concept quite so specific as abandonment. One can always rationalize a program or a building as contribution to the institutional health of the Church, to its glory and its upbuilding, even to "mission." But what happens when we admit to ourselves and the world that *abandonment* is an integral aspect of Christian mission? What happens when we apply the Protestant principle to institutional Protestantism?

The most difficult implementation of institutional abandonment will be at the local level, as churches are called upon literally to cease existing as institutions in order to create truly cooperative ministries. Perhaps the brief sketch we have drawn of what a cooperative ministry might look like will suffice to start some congregations on the road to institutional abandonment for the sake of mission. Certainly there is sentiment among the clergy and the laity for such an approach. Nonetheless, what is asked is much. The risks and threat implied in the very meaning of renewal will be felt as profoundly in the restructuring as in the new, more exposed forms of the Church that emerge from the ashes of the old. The notion of abandonment makes such risk clear. It offers no hiding place.

The first principle of institutional abandonment is that the Church should distinguish as wisely as possible between programs that are serving the unmet needs of mankind and those which are repeating the work of secular agencies. Is it wise, for example, to maintain extensive financial investments in homes for the aged, colleges, community centers, and other institutions which repeat functions that are carried on perfectly well by the government and private enterprise? Would the relatively limited funds of the churches not be better spent in experiments in these areas which do not duplicate existing services?

Too often the churches take advantage of their tax-exempt status to build institutions that not only compete with but mirror the standards of both the private and public sectors

of the economy. A critical survey of Protestant church building for the elderly, for example, would probably reveal that
the facilities serve primarily middle-class white church members and are essentially similar to those offered by commercial companies. In many cases, one imagines, there is even a
profit involved, though of course it is plowed back into the
institution rather than distributed to stockholders. Does
this mean the Church should not be involved with the
elderly? Of course not, but it ought to involve itself in
one of two ways—in experimenting with new and more
humane forms of planning for the aged which might serve
as models for the total society, or by filling desperate needs
that are not being met either by government or private
enterprise.

The basic principle is this: *Do not offer duplicate services.
Do not take secular powers off the hook by offering just
enough to excuse major involvement on the part of the total
society.* (One suspects that the well-meant paternalism that
has retarded the progress of inner-city residents is a direct
result of the old-style church-sponsored settlement house.
Similarly, the nation's skid rows have been left to the Salvation Army.) If the old institutions of social service are to
be maintained by the Church, they must now be transformed into pilot projects or unusual centers of social witness, experimentation, or service to unmet needs.

A good example of the abandonment of a church-related
institution to social struggle is Tougaloo College near Jack-
son, Mississippi. Its affiliation with the United Church of
Christ and its social position in Mississippi give it a crucial
role in the civil rights struggle. But there is no real reason
why most church-related colleges need remain so, unless
they fulfill one of the criteria of institutional abandonment.

A corollary to this is that the Church ought to allow for
the termination of its various social service projects, making

provisions for this in its actual institutional makeup. The Church should not avoid long-term commitments, but like a good foundation, it should be more concerned with starting something than with maintaining it after it has proved its value to humanity.

A good example of this principle at work is the Community Renewal Foundation in Chicago. It was started as a program of the Chicago City Missionary Society. Its aim is to exert a creative influence on housing in the city. After a short time it became apparent that such a program would have to be built around a far broader base than the Missionary Society could provide. The Society willingly provided funds to enable the Community Renewal Foundation to become a separate institution, operating with an interfaith board, and receiving foundation and government funds. It is now playing a highly constructive role, not only in influencing urban renewal and building sorely needed middle-income housing, but in providing legal services to the poor and renovating slum buildings. The primary role of the Society was to provide initial funds to enable an imaginative Episcopalian layman to implement his ideas about housing. By consciously exempting the program from typical forms of institutional allegiance (such as using the Society's name) and at the same time pushing the project toward structural involvement with other agencies, the Society's role was essentially that of research and development for the whole metropolitan Church. Thus a general rule of thumb might be that no program within Protestantism receive church funds for more than three years without a thorough re-evaluation. Hiring ought to be done on a similar basis. In a decentralized Protestant structure these concepts would be likely to operate much more effectively than at present.

5

What are we to say of the more unpopular or misunderstood aspects of abandonment? How is the Church to serve the needs of small numbers of persons—artists in the metropolis for example—when a majority of church members can see no "results" or no value in such a ministry? How can a number of highly specialized and not widely accepted ministries (some of them quite expensive to operate) take place within the democratic, locally based structure we have outlined? We have already defined a willingness to experiment and risk as an attribute of abandonment. But who will stand up for the Church's talented young rebels, or for highly skilled lay persons, such as the director of the Community Renewal Foundation? Who will support the Church, insofar as it is, in Harvey Cox's phrase, "God's *avant garde*"?

I think the only answer can be the creation of certain autonomous funding agencies from region to region. They would have the independence to finance a project that might initially prove too expensive or otherwise undesirable for the cooperative ministries. In order that this proposed independent agency be responsible to the churches in the region, there ought to be an attempt to encourage eventual administration and, when possible, support of experiments by the local churches after a reasonable length of time. Such agencies might also handle contingency funds to meet special needs of the local churches. Such funding agencies already exist in embryonic form. The various mission and missionary societies now operating with relative autonomy in Chicago, New York, Boston, and San Francisco (the Glide Foundation) could be prototypes of this suggested structure.

6

The possibilities of abandonment, once Protestantism is institutionally equipped to venture forth, are limitless. *Abandonment of* becomes *abandonment to*—the racial struggle, the effort to find human solutions to automation, the arts, the struggles of youth, the search for authentic vocational commitment amid centralized bigness, political problems, and one thousand other areas where life is lived. Once we have secured a streamlined institutional base for the Church, built around chaplaincy and teaching, we can respond heartily to Gordon Cosby's vision of the Church on mission in the world.

Abandonment would take the form, first, of listening, of exposure, and then of appropriate action. Since we are entering a metropolitan era, it is in the metropolis that we are most likely to learn the shape of our abandonment. We shall find, in any examination of urban specifics, that there are numerous junctures at which a restructured Protestantism could play a servant role. But since this servant role could be misinterpreted as merely being a perpetuation of the "soup kitchen" missionary work that has characterized the Church's past approach to the metropolis, I shall offer here a brief survey of urban concerns which may illuminate new possibilities for engagement. The list is necessarily selective, but it points to needs which are not being met and, in many cases, to needs which suggest definite abandonment ministries.

a) City Government

Compared to the federal government, the structures of city governments are diverse, complex, and often baffling.

The task of running a city on a purely technical level—sanitation, water supply, transportation, building codes, etc.—is in itself very involved. The location of political power, the effort to determine who makes what happen and how, is a task requiring intensive investigation. The federal division of authority into three power structures—the legislative, executive, and judicial—is not followed on the city level. In some cities, like Chicago, the lion's share of power rests with the mayor, who is elected by all the people. The city council, elected by the various local machines under the mayor's control, serves as a rubber stamp for the mayor. This is a problem in itself. City judiciaries are overlapped by a complex court structure which stretches from a local police court to the numerous criminal and civil, county, state, and federal courts leading finally, though rarely, to the United States Supreme Court. In many cities the local, and even the state, judiciaries are influenced by the machine and thus fail to perform a rightful role as a check on concentrated authority.

The common conclusion of many urban residents is the doleful admission: "You can't fight city hall." It might be amended to read: "It's difficult to fight city hall through the orderly processes of government." One reason why this is so is that most cities tend to follow a pattern of monolithic, one-party rule. In practically every large city it can be assumed that the administration will rest with the Democrats. An elaborate system of patronage serves to concentrate this authority even further. Through the medium of patronage, by which victorious political parties can dispense various municipal jobs, the party in power can command the resources—and cash—of every job holder at election time to insure its self-perpetuation. The power of the ballot in the metropolis seems to emerge as a weak instrument. So long as the machine can avoid major scandals, it can run the

government with little threat of competition. Now it is true
that monolithic city governments, built as they must be on
a maze of technical needs from sanitation to paved streets,
may serve the community well, or at least a substantial majority of the community. But the growing problem in the
city is to give expression to the will of its substantial minorities.

In past times the European minority groups, especially
the Irish and Italians, were eventually assimilated into the
mainstream of city life and society, in some cases even
taking over the machinery of government. But Negroes and
Puerto Ricans, who form the leading minorities in many of
today's American cities, have not achieved the same opportunities and acceptance as former migrants to the city. Without elaborating the numerous obvious and not so obvious reasons for this, it can be stated that these substantial minorities
are relatively voiceless in most city governments. Thus these
minorities have taken to the streets to express their dismay
with the city fathers, whether in school boycotts, demonstrations of the poor seeking increased welfare benefits, or
even demonstrations designed to change parking regula-
tions. Political scientists might spend some time reflecting on
the increasing truth that the shortest way to the mayor's
office is to have a demonstration which is carried on television and thus witnessed by the publicity-conscious city
administration.

Without considering the problem of city government in
depth, some questions can be raised. How are checks and
balances to be achieved in cities where government rests on
a monolithic political machine? How are the rights of
minorities to be maintained through government channels?
What possibilities exist for placing most city jobs on a non-
partisan merit employment system? What are the possibilities of creating effective forms of neighborhood expression

in the large cities? Is there any point in separating the political and technical functions of city government? How
reliant are cities on the benignity of state legislatures? How
can city governments pay their way without reversing the
flow of personal and commercial wealth away from the
city's center? Laymen freed from ushering might tackle
these questions.

b) Governing the Metropolis

The emerging metropolis embraces far more space than
that circumscribed by the corporate limits of major cities.
The New York Metropolitan Area, for example, includes
countless suburban towns and cities in New York State
plus the urbanized territory of two adjacent states, New
Jersey and Connecticut. The totality and interdependence
of this area is acknowledged in various cooperative enterprises. But coordinated planning and development of the
region—which is needed to create a livable metropolis in
the future—is still far from realized. Some cities, like Nash-
ville, Tennessee, have merged county and municipal government into what is called "metropolitan government."
But Chicago's metropolitan region exemplifies the potential problem faced by cities unable to coordinate their planning with the suburbs. It is estimated that the population
of the city of Chicago will increase by only 5 per cent in the
next thirty years; Chicago's suburbs are expected to more
than double their population in the same period. One Chicago area planner, speaking of the suburbs, notes: "We're
worrying about running short of water; at the same time,
we're worrying about being flooded out. We're worrying
about becoming industrialized and urbanized; at the same
time we're worrying about becoming overtaxed. We're
worrying about becoming polluted; we're worrying about
losing mass transit, even temporarily. And we're worried

about having to live on little pieces of land in between inter-
changes in the highway network." *

It may seem inconsistent to point to the monolithic character of municipal government while suggesting a greater
concentration of power over the total metropolitan area,
but there are certain factors that point to positive aspects
of "metropolitan government." One is that the inclusion of
suburbia in the urban political unit would tend to reactivate
the two-party system, so sadly missing in most of our cities.
Today, Republicans tend to concentrate in the suburbs, bliss-
fully unaware of the potentialities of rapid urbanization.
Democrats are mostly in the city limits. The political merg-
ing of these two areas might serve to create responsible debate about the future of the total region rather than scattershot efforts to preserve individual interests. The emergence
of such phenomena as suburban slums should give pause
to those who feel that the suburb and city share no common
problems.

The discussion of city and metropolitan government
should intensify certain questions which will have to be
answered in the course of deciding the nation's political and
sociological future: How can a sense of local imagination
and initiative be maintained in the face of complex, corporate decision-making? What reforms seem necessary to
increase the effectiveness of local government? What are the
rights of individual property owners in the development of
the metropolis? What steps can be taken to educate the
public to the implications of urbanization? Again, the restructured Church could wrestle with these issues.

c) The Schools

The full burden of public education has yet to be assumed
by the American people, and nowhere is this more evident

* Robert Morris in James Twomey's "The Two Sides of Howard Street," *Renewal*, December 1962, p. 6.

than in the big cities. (The depressed rural areas are also victimized by educational unconcern, which, because of the migration of the rural poor to the cities, intensifies the urban problem.) In plain terms, Americans are simply not willing to pay the costs of public education. Automation is making certain forms of education obsolete, and racial problems have further mobilized public hostility toward the educational enterprise. No American institution is more debated, more important and, at the same time, more undernourished. When daring bond issues, designed to create imaginative, large-scale programs of education, are needed, we find urban school boards hesitant to propose bond issues even for minimal programs. The unwillingness of the American public to pick up the educational tab (despite the fact that college is billed as "America's best friend") is easily documented. It has been demonstrated (see Patricia Sexton's book *Education and Income*) that the quality of schools supported from the same tax base almost always varies with the income level of student families. Thus, in inner-city areas children simply do not get the advantages offered in a public school in a wealthier neighborhood. Teachers are reluctant to accept the risks of teaching in the more "dangerous" neighborhoods. There is talk of special programs and of compensating teachers for the extra effort it takes to help deprived children, but it is mostly just talk. Negro parents have demonstrated, through boycotts, their dissatisfaction with school segregation. But the plain truth is that they are demonstrating primarily against inferior education. The Negro sees education as one of the few tickets of admission to first-class citizenship, and inferior schools simply overtax the frustration of parents determined that their children escape the web of despair they have known.

School boards and school administrators have fallen down

on the job when they have failed to alert the general public to the obsolescence of much present-day education. There are certain methods of upgrading the quality of education. Standardized achievement tests can mobilize public opinion in school areas where performance is low. Increased vocational training with contemporary equipment can help fill the job void created by automation. Teaching can be upgraded both as a public service and as a source of income. But in the last analysis no progress is possible without funds, and America's love of the automobile (witness highway budgets) and of overkill capacity (witness defense statistics) takes precedence over her love for education, at least when that love is translated into practical commitment. The present correlation of income and education only serves to perpetuate the downward spiral of dependency and unemployment that gives substance to Michael Harrington's thesis in *The Other America*. The increased inability of Roman Catholics to support the expensive parochial school structure is another challenge which must be faced. The unwillingness of some Protestants to compromise on the matter of federal aid to education is a second road block. The tendency toward higher salaries for administrators than teachers is another evidence of the current problem. Surely the ministries of abandonment could begin to focus on these issues— both through the creation of lay task forces and through educational experiments designed to provide additional options to those presently available.

d) *Welfare*

The English Reformation Statute of 1536 decreed that every child of the poor be removed from his home at the age of five and sold as a servant. America's Puritan founders condemned paupers to social ostracism. Not until August 14, 1935 did a comprehensive measure—the Social Security Act

—designed to tackle the problem of poverty, become law. Even then the existence of poverty was regarded as a temporary phenomenon. Among the world's wealthiest nations, the United States remains reluctant to take full-scale steps to alleviate the plight of the poor. Perhaps this is due to the Puritan heritage with its emphasis on work as an emblem of salvation. It is also due to the present unwillingness of many Americans to bear the moral responsibilities of affluence.

Cook County, home of Chicago, serves as a case to illustrate the dimensions of the public welfare problem in our large cities. Over $14,000,000 each month is needed to provide for the more than 225,000 persons on relief in Cook County. About 45 per cent of this cost is borne by the federal government, the rest by the state. Twelve out of 25 persons on public assistance in the county are children; and only five are able-bodied men who could, with training, be employed. The state of Illinois has consistently tried to keep welfare payments on a subsistence level. At one point fresh milk was banned from the tables of welfare recipients. When federal social security rates were hiked, state welfare payments were reduced. Relief recipients complain that clothing expenses and other "incidentals" required to keep children in school force them to cut into money allotted for food. Food appropriations are already lower than the subsistence budget projected by the U.S. Department of Agriculture. Downtown Chicago has been the scene of Marches of the Poor, designed to create a public opinion that will substitute a policy of rehabilitation, or, better, a guaranteed annual income, for the present policy of punishing the poor for their poverty.

The "welfare" issue evokes much heated debate. Biblical quotations about considering the industry of the noble ant are placed alongside injunctions to relieve the needs of a neighbor in distress. And yet, along with schools, welfare emerges as an important factor in the American debate: whether to devise the means to give all persons equality of opportunity or to perpetuate the popular belief that anyone who decides to can get ahead by sheer will power.

The outcome of the "war on poverty" will have tremendous consequences for the future life of the metropolis. Cities now tend to become repositories of the poor. Huddled into ghetto neighborhoods, the poor—most of them Negro—are faced with the prospect of never-ending dependency. Their presence and their growing numbers represent a threat to urban stability. Their desperation is reflected in everything from crime and narcotics addiction to spontaneous violence. Theologian-lawyer William Stringfellow, a resident of New York City, has predicted that the prospect of continued joblessness—hence of increased welfare—combined with frustration about race prejudice, is creating a situation in which prolonged, frequent outbursts of spontaneous violence can be anticipated throughout the cities of the United States. Recent outbreaks in New York and Los Angeles may be only a beginning. It is safe to say that the present, penny-wise and pound-foolish approach to welfare is creating the breeding ground for such outbursts.

Cook County Director of Public Aid, Raymond Hilliard, a harsh critic of the punitive approach to poverty, offered the following estimate of the costs of a program that might serve to rehabilitate welfare recipients: "Take the year ahead in Chicago. We will spend in the neighborhood of $200,000,-000 in relief grants and the amount will rise if poverty increases. To attack poverty in Chicago, which is costing such great and needless sums in relief grants, would involve dealing with about 50,000 family heads, a group of manageable size, and preparing them through education chiefly for a transition from dependency into independence and the pride of self-support.

The education would cost (for 20,000 of the 50,000 this coming year)	$1,300,000
Abolition of discrimination in hiring would cost	Nothing
Abolition of underemployment would cost	Nothing
Letting Negroes live where they wish would cost	Nothing
Open occupancy would cost	Nothing

The price is right; the time is right. If the forces of righteousness and enlightenment will take the field, there can be for the poor people of America a new life, new horizons, new hopes." * Earlier in his statement, Mr. Hilliard had expressed hope that religious groups might aid in the public education needed to implement such a transition. Again a ministry of abandonment is suggested.

e) Public Housing

The "answer" to slums in many large cities has been the construction of public housing. Public housing projects are usually concentrated in, or at the fringe of, ghetto areas; the architecture tends to be high-rise; and the reaction to public housing has varied from the observation that the projects are better than slums to the accusation that they themselves are vertical slums. Chicago's projects house 138,-000 persons in 28,750 living units. One Chicago project, the Robert Taylor Homes, has 28 sixteen-story, high-rise buildings housing 27,000 persons, 20,000 of whom are children.

* Renewal, June 1963, p. 13.

The Taylor complex is flanked by expressways on one side and a slum on the other. It is one block wide and two miles long. The implications of such an incredible concentration of persons in such a uniform setting have yet to be fully determined. Median annual income of Chicago's public housing families is $3,400. The pattern in Chicago is repeated in other large cities, New York being another example of the concentration of such housing in ghetto neighborhoods.

The reason for public housing is quite simply the inability of many urban families to pay the prices required by the private housing market. Thus, within the city there may be numerous vacancies in so-called stable neighborhoods, while the ghettos teem with those unable to pay rent or lacking the proper skin coloration to be accepted in other neighborhoods despite ability to pay. There are, of course, alternatives to the present tendencies in public housing. It may become possible to create smaller concentrations of public housing—with emphasis on row houses instead of high-rises—if neighborhoods can be induced to accept such housing in their midst. The possibilities of rent subsidies to enable persons of low income to afford the private housing market are also being explored. The present form of public housing is an invitation to urban disaster. The most deprived members of society are concentrated into small, impersonal boxes in the tradition of the old poorhouses. They see almost no chance of upward mobility. They are in a continual state of ambivalence—whether to make the best of what they have or to seek to break through the barriers which public housing represents. Is public housing a permanent way of life or a way station on the road to better things? It is conceivable that public housing residents may someday organize in large numbers to express their frustration with the status quo.

A former public housing manager has given a candid picture of life within the projects in *Renewal,* September 1964: "The elevators become the focal toy, the stairwells the chief meeting place. . . . Since everyone is a stranger, a stranger from outside the project is not recognized, so the elevators, stairwells, hallways, and streets become doubly dangerous. . . . Meanwhile the tenant, with great hope, moves out of his roach-and-rat-infested firetrap into an apartment where his next-door neighbor is the thickness of one porous concrete block away. He moves into a bewildering array of rules concerning rent payments, income limitations, garbage disposal, use of laundry facilities, control of children, cooperative sweeping of lobbies, etc. None of these rules did he help to frame." Indeed this is the problem noted by almost every sensitive observer of the public housing scene. The dominant atmosphere of depression comes primarily from the fact that all sense of self-determination is missing. The public housing resident feels he has no voice, no power, no place to move. The problem is intensified by the city's unwillingness to create the environmental possibilities inherent in scattered sites and rent subsidies. A unified, local cooperative ministry could prepare the way for a more human approach to housing.

f) *Urban Renewal*

Urban renewal is a process by which cities cooperate with the federal government in financing the physical, and hopefully the human, upgrading of city neighborhoods. Ideally urban renewal requires the participation of the persons in the areas to be "renewed," though this has not always been so. In one Chicago neighborhood countless homes were bulldozed to make room for a university campus, despite the strenuous objections of long-time residents. In general, the "successful" urban renewal programs have taken place in middle- to upper-middle-class neighborhoods where a large measure of private initiative has supplemented the financial help of the government. This means that urban renewal programs, despite their obvious benefits, have tended to help those who were already helping themselves and to neglect persons in the city's most needful areas. The two primary renewal programs in Chicago, for example, were in the city's sophisticated Hyde Park-Kenwood community, where the University of Chicago is located, and in Lincoln Park, where the populace tends to be made up of well-off professional persons. Directly adjacent to both these areas are slums and Negro ghettos that have had no urban renewal.

Some private developers have taken advantage of urban renewal to build projected "middle-income" apartment buildings which subsequently turn out to be "luxury" buildings. Chicago's Carl Sandburg Village, built on land that had been acquired and cleared by the government, billed itself as a middle-income development for families. But when completed, rents for a two-bedroom apartment—the largest available in the high-rise buildings—began at $240 a month with a limitation of four persons to an apartment. This was a far cry from middle-income rentals. In short, urban renewal has tended to benefit the wealthy rather than the poor. It is of great value in insuring the investments of the "haves," but it does little for the "have nots."

Some modest, but encouraging, developments have taken place to improve urban renewal. One is the provision in the Federal Housing Act that enables private, nonprofit agencies (such as churches) to build middle-income housing with the help of favorable, low-interest loans from the government. The great need in our cities is for housing that can be afforded by persons in the $5,000-$9,000 income bracket. The growth of a middle-income housing program is one key to meeting this need. Another is the inclusion in urban renewal plans of provisions for the construction of scattered-site, small public housing in urban renewal areas. This development will tend to alleviate the current malaise of public housing and to integrate city neighborhoods both racially and economically. The involvement of many church groups in this approach to housing would be both feasible and worthy.

g) *Transportation*

Someone should use a tape recorder to record the traffic report that one hears on every big city radio station during rush hour: "Traffic is backed up two miles on the F.D.R. Drive; there has been an accident on Bruckner Boulevard; drivers would be better off to avoid the Triboro Bridge." Such bulletins are commonplace, and should prove humorous to future generations unless, of course, nothing is done within the near future to alleviate the traffic problems of the metropolis. It is safe to predict that the prohibition of cars from the city will be a useful campaign issue for some future candidate for city office. With few exceptions our cities are woefully inadequate in provisions for high-speed public transportation. The New York rush hour—with its sardinelike concentration of humanity in countless hot subway cars and the crush of automobiles on the highways—is a classic picture of the present transportation problem, rivaled only by the spectacle of freeway traffic in Los Angeles. The choicest real estate in the central city is now gobbled up by entrepreneurs who can charge up to five dollars a day for the privilege of parking an automobile after the nerve-shattering trek from the suburbs. It is certain that a nation that can send space ships into the stratosphere can, with small effort, devise modern transportation for the metropolis. It is to be hoped that such transportation will be an alternative to the continued construction of expressways which fragment the urban area and divide neighborhoods. The ultimate expression of the dehumanization implied by the expressway was the attempt, in recent years, to push a road through the one patch of greenery—Washington Square Park—in New York's Greenwich Village. The outraged citizenry won the battle.

One solution to the traffic jam that is strangling our cities would be the separation of automobile from pedestrian traffic; another would be the encouraging of the bicycle as a means of local transportation and the provision of safe thoroughfares for bicycle riding. Monorails and other imaginative conveyances might be tried. The expense would be great, but the price of current trends in urban transportation is incalculable. But who in the metropolis will fight the battle for change?

h) Recreation and Culture

One of the consistent attractions of the big city, historically at least, has been the variety and scope of recreation available there. It is in the big city that life in the grand manner is possible, from New York, with its cotillions for the children of the well-off, to San Francisco, with its emphasis on lavish city homes. The stately shops of Fifth Avenue, the various clubs for gentlemen that dot the big cities, the theaters and concerts, the big-league teams, the first-run movies—all have contributed to the city's reputation as a center of leisure and recreation. Then, too, the city has been a place where most persons have been able to maintain their anonymity, thus enabling them to sample pleasures without the censure of a next-door neighbor or watchful small-town gossip. Museums and galleries are in the big cities, as are penny arcades and burlesque shows. Amusement parks and skating rinks, coffee shops and sightseeing attractions also contribute to the city's reputation as a recreational center. Then, too, there is the purely physical need for exercise which cities have tried to meet with the construction of parks. A glance at the Yellow Pages in any large city reveals the ingenuity of those whose business is the entertainment, stimulation, and amusement of the public. Here we touch upon one characteristic that makes cities exciting and desirable as a place to live. Within walking distance of my Chicago apartment is a great park, complete with a fine zoo, playing fields, a beach, and a botanical garden. A theater flourishes there in summer. Slightly farther away, but easily reached by foot, are coffee houses, interesting stores, various national restaurants. A further walk brings one downtown, where theaters, museums, a symphony orchestra, and summer band concerts are all to be found. These are some of the reasons why my personal prejudice is with the city.

As the strip city develops, with its highway culture, I suspect that we will see a growing lack of diversity in recreational facilities. Already the drive-in theater and the bowling alley seem the staples of suburban recreation. But on the other hand the opportunities exist for the creation of indigenous cultural enterprises in suburbia, ranging from the sponsorship of coffee houses where people can gather to talk and sing, to the establishment of theater groups. It is to be hoped that some order can be brought into the growth of the strip city to guarantee adequate open land for parks and camping facilities. If the United States landscape is increasingly marred by neon and signboard and gas-station architecture, the chances of making the urban regions into a fit habitation for men will be further diminished. And if the greed of real estate developers, in collusion with municipal governments, results in the gobbling up of available space, we can only be pessimistic about the future.

Leisure-time ministries may constitute a major focus of the ministry of abandonment.

i) Employment and Automation

The future of urban life, built as it is on technology and industry, will, in large measure, be dictated by how America deals with the impending problems posed by automation. There are two immediate problems. How can unskilled workers who are presently unemployed be retrained to take the numerous jobs that have been opened by automated technology? And what will be the situation if it is finally possible to eliminate all but the most skilled jobs? These questions have relevance not only for the blue collar worker but for the white collar man who may soon find a computer taking his place. Gerard Piel has added still other questions (*Renewal,* February 1964): "If a fraction of the labor force is capable of supplying an abundance of everything the population needs and wants, then why should the rest of the population have to work for a living? Preposterous alternatives come forward: give-away programs on television suggest that television might be employed to give the abundance away instead of trying to sell it. If production cannot be maintained at a profit under such circumstances, then why should a profit be made? Some other standard of accounting might serve even better to reduce waste and inefficiency. These questions are put in a deliberately extreme form. They suggest the kind of overturn in the values of our society which is already quaking the ground beneath our feet. The virtues of hard work and profit are rooted in scarcity. They have no relevance to the economics or the sociology of abundance."

It is not possible here to delve further into the complexities of automation with its potential displacement of workers on an unprecedented scale. The implication for the city is obvious; no longer is the city a place where the impoverished country residents can come with the hope of finding profitable, unskilled jobs. Even with retraining and a change in our educational system, the problem posed by Gerard Piel remains. The revolution in public mentality required to adjust to a technology of abundance is staggering. The solution to the problem posed by automation requires the entrepreneurial imagination of business, the foresight of government, and the willingness of the general public to consider the transmutation of three centuries of moral values. Until a viable solution is found, we can expect an increase in high-school dropouts, a rise in crime, continued growth of public welfare rolls, and, worst of all perhaps, the specter of a Negro community finally possessing its civil rights but without employment. It is an awesome prospect.

Parenthetically, in order to demonstrate the interdependence of practically every major problem in today's world, consider for a moment the implications of the pursuit of world peace for the metropolis. Should the government reduce its military spending in the future, the funds which would be released for public and private enterprise might begin to take up the slack in employment throughout the nation. It can be argued that the arms race contributes substantially to the creation of urban poverty and joblessness.

j) The Press

Under this heading I include daily newspapers and radio and television stations insofar as they deal with the life of the city where they are located. It is a commonplace in journalistic circles to note the way in which the press affects the making of news. The fact that television cameras are going to be present at a demonstration is, in itself, a pretext for demonstration. The role of the press in molding public opinion is a subject for continual research. One brief observation is that almost every problem highlighted in the press is a problem that has existed for some time without the attention of news media. Thus, when a headline reads: CRISIS IN COUNTY HOSPITAL, SYNDICATE MOVES AGAIN, or NEGROES VOICE GRIEVANCES, the chances are that each problem revealed "exclusively" by the press is the product of many years' making. Every three years a paper is more or less expected to "expose" crime, usually by publishing old pictures of mobsters' suburban homes. It will be noted that at the time of one mine disaster in Pennsylvania, similar disasters were reported throughout the world. It was no coincidence. Readers just happened to be interested in mine disasters. Other observations could be made. Newspaper reports of how demonstrations work in the South influence the conduct of mass movements in the North. The fact of self-immolation in Saigon breeds the threat of self-immolation in the cities of America. All this is merely a way of stating that the world is smaller and more interdependent.

The role of the press in the city is crucial. Despite the references to newspaper exposés, the crusading spirit has largely vanished from the city rooms of most papers. The city grows more complex, but the reporting of what is happening in the city becomes more superficial. Not one of Chicago's four major daily papers has taken a forthright position on the matter of welfare, education, or housing. Under the guise of objectivity, the news becomes vapid. The legwork of serious reporting is simply not done with the zeal that once animated journalists. This may sound like the nostalgic longing for the days of the muckrakers, but I honestly feel that it is the muckraking influence that is needed today, especially in the daily press. If justice is to reign over the life of our cities, we must be informed constantly about the city's problems, and we must be able to find in the newspapers a voice which speaks for the inter-

ests of those who are the casualties of rapid social change.
Papers have an opportunity not only to report, but to crusade—and crusade they must in order to prevent the complexity of city government from becoming a mask for the
deception and manipulation of the public. But has the
Church begun to minister to those who bear direct responsibility in the field of mass communications? How can the
Church teach them that there is a prophetic dimension to
their vocation?

7

The first thing the Church is free to do in tackling the
urban specifics (they can serve as an example of typical
areas of need) is to entrust the task of prophecy to the
trained laity. If the Church is ultimately people on mission,
it follows that the educated laity will operate most effectively within the natural environment of their everyday
associations. The last thing one should seek to create is
an artificial grouping of lay persons to issue moral pronouncements "as Christian businessmen." One need not
wear such a title on one's sleeve. No, the educated layman
is called to work within his sphere of influence in cooperation with other laymen to make the city as a whole more
human. Gradually in the metropolis a network of lay persons would develop through the structure I have outlined.
They might be presidents of companies or the inner-city unemployed. But they would become aware of their cumula-
tive power to change evil or outmoded structures and to
introduce human goals into the planning process. Metropolitan task forces would develop. The teaching arm of
the Church would serve as a resource, gathering material
to assist the laity in forming responsible conclusions and

strategies. If the task force were dealing with police problems, the metropolitan Church could call upon the right
laymen to work through the right channels.

Certainly this is one aspect of abandonment to the world
of the metropolis. The layman would be seen as one who
is *called to responsibility where he or she is located*. When
the city learns that good old-fashioned, respectable, don't-
rock-the-boat Protestantism has gotten a bit of savvy, that
it is willing to speak in the world's terms, and that its
primary interest is a humanized metropolis rather than
preferment for the Church, then some changes will be
forthcoming. When the bureaucratic structures of the
metropolis learn that the entire religious community has
forgotten differences and is united in favor of racial justice,
fair court procedures for the poor, decent housing for the
elderly, and equitable administration of building codes,
some heads will turn. When the laity realizes that its mission is in the world rather than in the church basement,
and when resource structures exist to clarify issues and
strategy, then the mission can begin.

In our hypothetical model of the cooperative ministry
we assumed that less than half the church membership
would be active in the local ministries of teaching, chaplaincy, and abandonment. Now one can see that active
church membership does not depend on participation in
the organized activities of the local church or even of the
local churches banded together cooperatively. One is an
active church member when one abandons one's self to the
human causes of the world.

One might suggest at this point that we are merely para-
phrasing two principles that have always been part of
Protestant understanding. The first is the *priesthood of all
believers*, which maintains that one can fulfill his mission
or priesthood regardless of one's occupation. The second

is what has been called the *Protestant ethic of work*, the Puritan notion that success in one's work is somehow a badge of salvation. Both principles need drastic overhauling if they are to be meaningful today.

It may be true that all Protestants are priests in a limited sense, but some are more priestly than others, and justifiably so. The notion of the priesthood of all believers tends to dull the legitimate authority of those entrusted with the mission of chaplaincy and teaching. It also tends to deify the individual conscience to such an extreme that anyone's interpretation of Scripture, for example, is regarded as justifiable. In the hurry to doff the pretensions of Renaissance Catholicism, Protestants managed to propound doctrines that, in their own way, were equally pretentious. The layman who says, in response to certain questions, "That's a matter for my minister to handle" is not always evading responsibility. He is recognizing the diversity which is necessary if the Body of Christ is to live in the world.

The Protestant work ethic is another approach that could use some revising. The notion that success (honestly gained and prudently invested) is tantamount to salvation may have had a lot to do with the rise of capitalism, but it is less than appropriate as a world view today. For one thing, we are already in the midst of an era when hard work is scarcely even required in the old sense of the phrase. Machines that will replace white collars, abundance that will make give-aways superfluous, and reverse incomes taxes are among the few tentative ideas that have emerged from contemporary discussions about cybernetics, *et al*. The normative notion in business today suggests more the responsible manager who owes his "success" as much to specialized training as to any inherent virtue or overwhelming initiative. The idea that financial success is a sign of salvation is, in itself, rather repugnant. One would not eliminate Aristotle Onas-

sis, Jean Paul Getty, and H. L. Hunt from the scope of
divine concern, but they may be no more resourceful or hard
working than the welfare-recipient mother who spends
sixty of the eighty dollars she gets for furniture on clothing
so her kids can go to school.

Our concept of the layman at work in the world goes
beyond the idea of the man or woman who is honest on
the job and nice to his or her colleagues. It assumes a new
sophistication at all levels of society and an increased awareness of the interdependence of all the elements of the world.
The layman is called to recognize his legitimate power
within this interdependent framework. If he works in the
field of communications, we are not interested in harnessing his talent to fill institutional goals of the Church. We
are pleased if he can use his skill creatively on the job. *But
our primary concern is that he employ his talent to make
the total machinery of society more humane and livable.*
It is our hypothetical layman in newspapers, radio, or TV
who might be called to waken the mass media to unjust
situations or to offer his talent as a consultant to, or par-
ticipant in, a ministry of abandonment.

8

At the outset we substituted the terms chaplaincy, teaching, and abandonment for the traditional terms *kerygma,
diakonia,* and *koininia.* It may be said that we have dealt
with *kerygma* (proclamation) and *diakonia* (service) in
the new structure we have proposed, but what of the
koininia, the community? It is my belief that we must be
as experimental in our understanding of community as in
our understanding of proclamation and service. There are
at least four sociological marks of community: local loyalty,

consensus, shared life, and dedication to something larger than the group. In the presently structured Church we tend to lack consensus, primarily because the denominational congregation is unable to do all that must be done, and its unity may well be shattered if it is given too many imperatives. In the proposed structure there would be a recognition of a time and place for everything, of the need for various sorts of consensus existing in creative tension, one with another, in the cooperative ministry. Today the tension in local congregations is not creative but destructive. It stems more from a sense of impotence than of possibility. So the differentiation inherent in the new structure is itself likely to increase the possibility of community.

One might argue that local loyalty exists in today's local congregations, but we have seen that they are tied to national denominations and at the same time so burdened with institutional demands that they scarcely have the energy to look at the neighborhood in which they exist. Local loyalty emerges primarily when local residents feel they can contribute positively to the life of the neighborhood. Despite a needed emphasis in recent years on transcending narrow community self-interest, I feel strongly that local loyalty of certain types is most desirable as an antidote to the centralized, bureaucratic, impersonal administration that seems to be engulfing most of American society. Seen in this light, local loyalty can be a radical social force rather than a regressive one. Indeed the most progressive movements of our time have recognized that it is no longer possible to solve problems without involving the persons whose problems are supposedly being addressed. As we have seen, this lies behind the notion of the participation of the poor in the war on poverty, behind the most exciting notions of community organization, and behind the most advanced ideas on urban planning which insist on the restoration of

human values within our presently sprawling cities. The restructured Church would, of course, transcend the neighborhood. It would also be truly loyal to the neighborhood, and
this would measurably add to the growth of a sense of community within the Church.

The ministries of abandonment suggest to me a shared
life both at the local level and the metropolitan level. Here,
instead of small groups whose function is merely to perpetuate themselves, we have groups called together to work
for something beyond the group. Certainly the abandonment ministries might, in themselves, aim at creating new
structures of community in the metropolis, new structures
of living together. For example, why couldn't interested lay
persons purchase housing where they would live, but which
they could also rent out for purposes of creating true diversity in their communities? New forms of shared family
existence—families maintaining a common house or apartment for weekday child care or even preschool activities—
could contribute models which might be followed by the
world as a whole. Again the inventiveness and potential
mobility for action of the dedicated local community would
be a happy alternative to the static structures of the present.

Certainly on the metropolitan level the cooperative ministries could themselves cooperate to bridge the racial and
economic barriers that threaten to make the United States
a scene of the most gruesome sort of guerrilla warfare if
nothing is done. No concept of abandonment that does not
deliberately facilitate communication between the various
ghettos (both rich and poor) of the modern metropolis is
justifiable.

Finally there is a sort of community that has no sociological explanation that can do it full justice. This is the
Pentecostal community of the gathered Church when it is
fully alive, singing and celebrating, sharing and marching,

responding with thanks to the wonders wrought by a reconciling grace that is happily beyond our control. The com-
placent Church is the true "death of God" movement. The
Church that is able to bring unity out of diversity in worship is the true house of the living God. And I would hope
that the centers of chaplaincy might contribute to the mira-
cle of Pentecost in our time. When I attend an Episcopal
Church I am denied the Pentecostal fervor of the Negro
Baptist Church; when I attend the Negro Baptist Church
I am denied the objective mystery and joy of the Sacrament.
And it will no longer do to say that I can work for change
in a single congregation because I know that the true
Pentecostal mystery will never be fully shared until the worship of the Church is itself allowed to flow together from
all the separate buildings where we hide the little light that
we have from ourselves and from the world.

9

It is obvious that an ecumenical Church, built around a
functional distinction between chaplaincy, teaching, and
abandonment, can perform such ministries far more effectively than today's truncated Protestantism. The power of
local ecumenicity has already been demonstrated sufficiently
to show forth its efficiency. The recent union of churches
in Rochester, New York, to start a controversial but necessary grass roots community organization in that riot-torn
city, is but a single example. The entire financial structure
of the Church that is ecumenically based enables the abandonment ministry to expand in direct relation to the voluntary involvement of laymen. The arduous process of debate
at the local level is ultimately preferable to the present practice of organizing groups of clergymen to fight battles that
should involve the entire Church. (To be fair to the clergy,

however, one should recognize that virtually no local debate could have occurred before their direct involvement in various struggles.)

The ministry of abandonment already exists in muted form within Protestantism. Despite the fact that the lion's share of church funds has gone into institutional maintenance, one would have to say that Protestant abandonment is currently more effective than Protestant ministries of chaplaincy and teaching. This is a damnable judgment to have to make, but it turns our gaze once again to the cumbersome inefficiency and lack of virility that pervade denominational Protestantism. The greatest cause for hope is that a recognition of abandonment as an essential ministry of the Church will force the Christian community to see how futile our social action is without a solid restructuring of the Church as chaplain and teacher. The renovation must be total!

I have tried in these pages to point a way out of the current Protestant dilemma. We live in a time when the present institutional structures of the Church are simply unable to fulfill the ministries which Christians are called to perform. Most observers are prepared to admit that denominationalism is obsolete. Most would not wish to see a regimented Protestantism run from the top down. Most are agreed that the Church has become too institutionalized, too concerned with its own survival. My attempt has been to suggest a few guidelines aimed at moving the Church from where it is to where it ought to be: squarely in the world of human need, but at the same time squarely committed to the teaching and proclamation of a Gospel that transcends all of history and is Good News to all men.

Perhaps it is too early to write a book such as this with its suggestion of a specific approach to the structural malaise

of the Church. But somewhere, sometime, the debate must
be brought into the open, the discussion of specifics must
begin. We must integrate our theological insights with
structural proposals, and we must begin to see the unrest of
ministers and laymen as a positive possibility. For out of
this integration of thought and action, out of this harnessing
of unrest, I am encouraged to hope that we may be on the
verge of a day of glory for the Church. It will not be a
day of self-congratulation but of profound praise. For having gained a specific vision (in Langdon Gilkey's phrase) of
how the Church can minister to the world without losing
itself, we shall be free to make the first tentative steps toward the recovery of the joy and the spirit of sacrifice appropriate to true Christianity.

We have passed through a decade of false religious revival. We have passed through five subsequent years of
carping and backbiting and discouragement with Church
structure, five years in which the most vital expression of
the Gospel was in the worship of men of many persuasions
in the prison cells of the South. Now it is time to start
walking toward the new structure; it is time to move on;
it is time to become the Church we claim to be; it is time
that Jesus Christ be mocked for the right reasons; it is time
to teach once more, to preach once more, and to walk the
Jericho Road once more. It would be pleasant to forget all
of the structural problems involved in a responsible approach to Church renewal, to venture each in our own way
into the wilderness where, at least, we would hear no more
vapid sermons, no more comforting charades. But that may
be the all-too-easy road today. And if, in the coming years, we
could truly revolutionize the structures of the Church, we
would find the wilderness soon enough, for the Church
would no longer be safe from the Gospel it so haltingly proclaims today.

Epilogue
A Conversation
With Myself

Q/ Aren't you proposing another denomination?

A/ No. I am trying to avoid precisely the sort of fragmentation that has been a typical feature of Protestantism. If nothing constructive is done within the present structures, if no real change occurs, I am afraid we shall see the growth of many little sects and offshoots composed of the anti-institutional types referred to in Chapter Two. The sectarian strategy seems to me to tend toward totalitarianism and inflexibility rather than toward pluralism and diversity. If nothing is done, it will mean that the failure of the denominations and the local churches has been responsible for fundamentally unconstructive sectarian reaction.

Q/ Aren't you incurably naïve? Knocking the denominations, etc.?

A/ It may seem so, but I suspect that a true grass roots movement which is a threat to the denominations will do more to get the denominations moving than the sort of back-corridor backbiting that is standard today.

163

Q/ I think you are interested only in political causes and that everything else you have written is simply aimed at making the Church into a social action agency.

A/ I think that the upheavals that are going to take place in the next century will hardly be affected by the Church. Even the structure I propose is not likely to have a substantial effect on the outcome. I am primarily interested in discovering whether there is anything within the Bible, within the Gospel, within our hymns and prayers, that is able to address man significantly today. I think there is, but I have a hard time finding it in today's Church. If I were interested only in social action I would forget the Church in a minute and plunge into either the peace movement or the civil rights movement exclusively.

Q/ You offered a short chapter on theology, on what can be believed. Is that all you can say?

A/ I would like to be able to say more. We are in a time of seeking and yet I feel we can begin to move beyond both liberalism and neo-orthodoxy. The direction is unclear, but it may involve a real consideration of the possibilities of realizing a transition within human nature in this world in the context of what may well be a fantastic upheaval in the next fifty or one hundred years. My vagueness at this point should be reason enough for silence until the ideas begin to form themselves more clearly.

Q/ You write about a renewal movement as if nothing were happening. Are you unaware of the constructive things that are going on at the local level today?

A/ Not entirely. In fact, they are the impetus of this book, even though they are not described here. I believe the exciting realities of local ecumenism that already exist are the prototype of the renewed Church. I believe they will grow in number. I believe they will finally work to transform the denominational pattern.

Q/ This is all very optimistic. What is the worst thing you could imagine that might take place within Protestantism?

A/ The worst thing would be the continued identification of the Gospel with the salvation of the Church as opposed to the world. This could lead, and is leading in some cases, to an imperialistic attempt to identify the Church with the White West in a world where the White West is a minority. The Church would then become even more parochial and closed and would ultimately provide the "spiritual" impetus for an arrogant and self-righteous stand of the White West against the rest of the world. This would be a tragedy, and at that point we would have to fight the Church in the name of the Church.

Q/ Who will organize the renewal movement?

A/ You will, if you want to. It must grow from the grass roots and it must not get institutionalized too soon. Let any reader, minister, or layman begin his or her own organizing, because the focus of organization is where *you* are.

Q/ What if the denominations don't budge?

A/ The cooperative ministry must then come first, but hopefully this conflict can be averted.

Appendix

To accompany this book, or perhaps as a preparation for it, I suggest that interested persons refer to the paperback *Who's Killing the Church?* a collection of articles that have appeared in *Renewal* magazine during the last three years. The book is available from the Chicago City Missionary Society, 19 South La Salle Street, Chicago, Illinois 60603, and is distributed to bookstores by the Association Press. In a sense *Who's Killing the Church?* provides documentation for some of the criticisms in this book as well as specific suggestions which supplement those in this volume.

Prior to the publication of this book, I published a preliminary statement of its basic themes in *Renewal*, February 1966 ("The Grass Roots Church: Manifesto for a Renewal Movement"). Since the Manifesto provoked immediate response both in the national press and among ministers and laymen throughout the United States, there may be some service in including it, with only minor revisions, in this Appendix. Those who have read the book will obviously find considerable repetition, but I hope this will be offset by the value of the short Manifesto as a possible rallying point for individuals and groups who wish to move along the lines suggested.

1. DENOMINATIONALISM. We believe that denominationalism is obsolete, both theologically and in terms of the capacity of denominations to organize the Church in the most

effective and obedient manner. We believe that participants in a renewal movement must openly express their willingness to forsake denominational loyalty at every point that such loyalty impedes the ecumenical witness of the Church, particularly at the local and metropolitan level. Denominationalism is theologically obsolete because it denies to all church members the total theological resources of all the denominations, forcing upon individual church members an intolerable choice of modes of worship and an equally intolerable allegiance to a fragment of the total Church. The denominations are structurally obsolete because they have turned into national bureaucracies, removed from local situations, which, by their very nature, impede the development of the Church's mission at the local level. We feel that the merger of denominations "at the top" is of value only if there is a radical transformation of the combined denominations to provide resources for local, ecumenical witness. While we appreciate the creative leadership at the top in many denominations, we see this leadership continually thwarted by the institutional demands of denominational self-preservation. Thus we have little hope in renewal movements aimed at restoring the life of individual denominations. Such movements are too easily domesticated. We advocate, as an alternative, the formation of a pandenominational grass roots organization of all persons, clergy and lay, who wish to fight for the Church structure which we shall propose.

2. THE THREE FUNCTIONS OF THE CHURCH. We believe that the Church has three tasks: Chaplaincy (the proclamation of the biblical insight into the human situation); teaching (the integration of this biblical insight with the realities of the contemporary world); and abandonment (the self-giving of the Church to the world). Chaplaincy refers to the priestly, liturgical, pastoral ministry of the Church. It is the ministry which today's seminaries claim to be preparing ministers to undertake. But the structure of today's Church leaves the clergyman with virtually no time to realize this essential ministry. Teaching has been utterly short-changed by the denominationally-organized Church, despite the massive investment of funds in sometimes

creative study materials, and the almost wasteful investment of local congregations in understaffed and underutilized educational facilities. The ministry of teaching requires specialized personnel, around-the-week facilities, and recognition by the Church-at-large as one of the Church's three essential tasks. Today the burden of teaching falls on ministers who already have too many responsibilities. The Church in its present structure offers virtually no training to adults. And the moribund quality of the instruction given to youth is partially attested to by the vast numbers of young persons who become disenchanted with the Church as soon as they leave home. The present understanding of the ministry and the present structure of the Church make a teaching ministry virtually impossible. Abandonment refers primarily to the Church's ministry to the world. It embraces specialized ministries aimed at making urban life more human, involvement of Christians in the social struggle, and the style of life that ought to become the distinguishing mark of individual Christians and the Church as an institution. Today the presently structured Church is so caught up in institutional maintenance that it cannot perform the ministries of teaching and chaplaincy. And, with the current, utterly inefficient emphasis on the denominational local congregation, virtually no funds exist to support specialized ministries of any sort. When a congregation cannot support the ministries of chaplaincy, teaching, and abandonment, it is both theologically and structurally irrelevant.

3. GOALS FOR THE RENEWAL MOVEMENT. The renewal movement should draw its theological rationale from St. Paul's missionary methods as outlined particularly in the First Letter to the Corinthians, chapters 12 and 13. Briefly St. Paul advocates that the Church is the Body of Christ. He states that the Body is made up of many parts, each one playing a specific function. In other words, he sees specialization—the division of responsibilities so that each function of the Church can be implemented—as essential to a healthy body. The absurdity of today's structure is revealed by the fact that we have lumped nearly every one of the tasks that Paul outlines into the job description

of the contemporary minister. This has led to a situation in which as many as two-thirds of the students in some seminaries indicate they cannot accept the present definition of the ordained ministry. The restructured Church will be based on a differentiation of function, on a recognition that some are called to preach, some to be prophets, some to be helpers, some to administrate, some to teach.

St. Paul also emphasizes, throughout his writings, that the local Church is the primary expression of the Body of Christ. If the local Church is not equipped properly, then it becomes irrelevant and incomprehensible. We can translate his concern into modern terms by saying that what must take place is a restructuring of the Church at the grass roots.

Another goal of the renewal movement will be the recovery of the total biblical understanding of the human situation. This means in our day that theology must be freed from the academic confines of the seminary and developed in the context of the active engagement of the Church in the world. In particular this means a recovery of the depths of the Old Testament, which at the dawn of Church history was the worship resource of the Church. God is not to be seen as having retired to some celestial lounging place after the advent of Christ, but rather as the brooding, active, argumentative, cajoling One who reveals Himself in history. Theologically, this means that we must become Jews in spirit before we can become Christians.

4. SPECIFICS. Since today's local denominational congregation can scarcely perform the functions which the Church is called to implement, we must arrive at a totally new understanding of the local congregation, based on a total restructuring of the Church at the local level. Since virtually no single congregation can support all three ministries—chaplaincy, teaching, and abandonment—we suggest the following elements of a new structure. First, local churches must band together to form cooperative ministries. Within a given cooperative ministry a single facility would be used for the ministry of chaplaincy. It would conduct services designed to offer the church member the full range of

Christian worship throughout the week, from the Episcopal liturgy to the silent meetings of the Quakers. Assuming that ten present-day congregations were involved in the cooperative ministry, possibly three facilities which now house congregations would be adapted for the teaching ministry of the restructured Church. They would be staffed by ministers and trained laymen who see their mission as teaching. In particular, every neighborhood would have a full-time facility for the training of adult laymen. The remaining buildings would be sold unless they could be easily adapted to the ministries of abandonment: that is, direct service to specific unmet needs in the community. (In no case should Church ministries of abandonment repeat what the secular world is already doing. They should aim at the unmet needs.) Each neighborhood would have a full-time center for pastoral counseling.

Theological seminaries would be called to restructure as follows: They would train men and women for specific ministries within the restructured Church. Some would be trained to preach, some to teach, some to counsel. The seminaries would also open their doors to the laity in the following way: The seminaries would agree to support the cooperative ministry concept by offering ten intern-year students and one professor to any cooperative ministry on an annual basis. In return, the given community would send ten laymen to the seminary. This would bridge the chasm which now exists between the seminary and the Church-at-large. Certain seminaries would be designated as centers of advanced theological study, and students inclined toward teaching careers could transfer to these centers if they felt called to do so.

Denominations would be called to restructure in the following manner: The bulk of current denominational expenditures are used for servicing the needs of local denominational congregations. This includes funding new church development projects, producing curriculum at the national level, and the support of local congregations that are unable to support themselves. We believe that all of these functions should be turned over, as much as possible, to the metropolitan and regional structures of the several denominations. This would include the transfer of church extension funds, funds for educational programs, and all other funds now used for the maintenance of local denominational programs. The denominations should, before turning these funds over, elicit an agreement that the local denominational units will use these funds on an ecumenical basis with other local denominational units. The basic principle informing the use of these transferred funds should be the priority of the cooperative ministry concept. We are calling here for the decentralization of approximately ninety per cent of current national programs conducted by denominations. We recommend that the national denominations see themselves in the future as research and development agencies serving the whole ecumenical Church. In particular we urge that endowments and other funds that could not legally be removed from the jurisdiction of national denominations be seen in the future as seed money for creative experimentation in areas that are beyond the purview of the proposed cooperative ministries. Denominations, shorn of many current institutional functions, would be free to concentrate on pilot projects, *ad hoc* experimentation, and on creative ecumenical projects that would still be needed on the national and international level.

The original purpose of denominations was to do what no single congregation could do for itself. Our proposal assumes that functions once carried out by denominations can most fruitfully be returned to the local level. We feel that the future of the denominations lies in experimentation, research, and development, and in serving the needs of a Church that would be truly ecumenical at its base.

We feel, in addition, that the distinctive theological contributions of individual denominations will be enhanced, rather than eliminated, in our proposed cooperative ministry structure. The worship of the cooperative ministry, in particular, would provide room for all legitimate traditions, because it would bring all the current resources of the denominations into a central worship facility serving the local neighborhood. We feel strongly that genuine dialogue at the local level is preferable to the creation of a routinized "ecumenical" theology forced upon the local churches from the upper echelons of Protestantism.

Thus our impatience with denominationalism is impatience with its present form and structure. We wish to free denominations for service, not to eliminate them.

Church membership would be redefined. One would become a member of the cooperative ministry and then, from year to year, would elect membership in one of the specialized ministries. Thus membership would refer both to confession of faith and mission in the world. The combining of present Church budgets at the local level would be more than enough to finance the cooperative ministries. Indeed, over half the funds could be available for outreach ministries, such as community organization.

The cooperative ministries would be the basis of the renewed Church. Essentially, the Church would then be organized along viable geographical lines. Since the metropolis is rapidly becoming the primary geographical unit in this country, any "superstructure" needed to support the local ministries or to carry on programs within the total area would be metropolitan and ecumenical, rather than national and denominational. Thus, we would come to refer to the Church in Chicago, the Church in New York, the Church in Boston, etc.

Within the metropolitan framework and the cooperative ministry structure, the number of ordained ministers needed would diminish by about half. Indeed, ordination would be reserved only to those with specific preaching and sacramental responsibilities. Thus as many as half of today's ministers would become laymen and an equal number of future seminary graduates would be laymen. This suggests that, with the emphasis on local and metropolitan training centers, the laity would become the prophetic arm of the Church. Laymen would regard the ministries of chaplaincy and teaching as fundamental resources and the ministry of abandonment as the fundamental expression of their faith in the world.

5. BEGINNING POINTS. You are invited to send copies of this proposal to key people in your denomination, asking for their consideration of it.

Attend denominational meetings to ask about the prospects for decentralization and grass roots ecumenical cooperation in your area.

Ministers in local areas should meet and publish their own "bill of rights," to indicate that they are no longer content with the job description of clergymen in the presently structured denominational Church.

Seminary students should consider the possibility of learning a "second skill" so that they will have an alternative to the ministry as it is presently defined, pending basic structural change.

Seminary faculties should initiate concrete debate on the role that seminaries can play in a cooperative, grass roots renewal movement.

The National Council of Churches should immediately consider means by which it can influence the denominations to decentralize and provide support for the cooperative ministry concept.

Laymen should initiate discussions of the cooperative ministry concept with their ministers.

Associate pastors and assistant pastors in local congregations should be freed of institutional responsibility to work with a special committee of laymen to determine prospects for a cooperative ministry in their area.

6. CONCLUSION. Our basic objective is not to create a hard and fast set of rules that apply to every situation, but to serve as a clearing house for the creative ideas of a renewal movement. Let our motto for the moment be: "The ecumenical movement must be local; the Body of Christ must incorporate specifically defined functions; and the renewed Church must be as faithful to the biblical reality that brings it into being as to the world that calls it into service." Above all, let us begin to substitute concrete, positive proposals for the carping and backbiting that characterize our existence in the outmoded denominational Church structure.